From the pit

TEARS

of JOY

God Bless

God Bless you~
and give you understanding,
hope and encouragement,
as you continue to trust
Him in you daily life
as He did me.
Sis in Christ,
Emma

EMMA HERNANDEZ

Tears of Joy
ISBN 0-88144-231-3
Copyright © 2006 by
Emma Hernandez
P. O. Box 892846
Oklahoma City, OK 73189-2846

Published by
Christian Publishing Services
P. O. Box 701434
Tulsa, OK 74170

Cover Design by Mary Adkins/GraphixStation
Text Design: Lisa Simpson

ACKNOWLEDGMENTS

Special thanks to. . .

My beloved Lord Jesus Christ, who, by His unconditional love for me, had His hand upon me and never let me go. Every day that goes by, early in the morning, noon, or at night, I thank God for loving me, saving me, delivering me out of the pit, and healing me. He is restoring me and has given me a new life. I felt like I was on death row! It's hard to truly express the love I feel for my Savior and Redeemer. He is my everything, my all, my peace, love, and joy forevermore. Thank You, Jesus, for Your mercy and grace that You extend to us.

My husband, Oscar, who has stood by me during the difficult years. I have gained greater love and admiration for you because of your sacrificial love.

Mrs. Mary Adkins, my beautiful daughter, for spending time designing and illustrating the cover of my book, but most importantly, for your support and prayers. I know that God heard your desperate prayer for me at a critical time in my life and He answered you.

There were several wonderful Christian friends who edited my book for me: Judy Baine, Gloria Cox, and Rev. Larry Woody, who declared to me, "Sister Emma, I believe you have a story to tell!" With encouragement and wisdom, I didn't give up this endeavor.

Again, my husband, Oscar, Mike Messel, Ken Shahan, Sue Bailey, Phyllis Baker, Zedna and Wayne Moore, and two cousins, Barbara and Gwen, for being instrumental in my conversion to Christianity. God used each of you, whether it was through prayer, prophecy, casting out devils, or laying on of hands, to accomplish His work in me, bringing me to salvation through Jesus Christ. I thank God for my own immediate family.

In many instances, God used my children – Tina Fortune, Tony, Michael, Mary, and Robert – in prayer or reading the Word of God over me to bring about my conversion. I thank God every day for our wonderful children and grandchildren. They are all a blessing from God to us. My other special, beautiful daughter, Tina, has blessed me so much with her prayers and daily support. I couldn't have asked for a more loving family.

I give thanks for my former pastors, as well as my present pastors, Spurgeon (Buck) and Juanita Jordan, and the congregation of Grace Chapel, Lexington, Oklahoma, for your loving support, both prayerfully and financially, in helping me to attain and remain faithful to the call of God on my life. May God's richest and abundant blessings come to you in every way!

CONTENTS

INTRODUCTION

This book is based on a true life story. It is a unique story unlike any another. No part of this book is fiction. However, I have changed the names to protect some people who are involved. Many facets of my own personal life are unveiled in this story.

Today, I am an ordained minister of the Lord Jesus Christ. I serve Him in missions in other countries like Mexico, Panama, and Honduras, sharing my testimony of what God has done in my life. I have been ministering to the women in prison in Lexington, Oklahoma, for fourteen years, and occasionally I minister in the Texas and Mexico prisons as well. I speak at women's conferences and wherever God opens the door to me.

God made a covenant with me, one of life and peace. He gave it to me that I might fear (reverence), respect, and honor Him. The law of Truth is in my mouth. I walk with Him in peace and equity and have turned many away from iniquity, for I am a servant of the Lord of Hosts. God created me to become a mother, not only of five children, but a spiritual mother of others as well.

I lived in spiritual bondage as a Jehovah's Witness for over thirty-three years. I was a victim of a date rape while in my teens. A curse of witchcraft was against my life, which caused me to live in tremendous fear nearly every night for over twenty-one long, miserable, and tormenting years. Suffering a stroke and a heart attack caused by a beating, led me to go through an out-of-body spiritual experience.

I had low blood sugar (hypoglycemia) and ulcers for over twenty-one years. And like Mary Magdalene in the Scriptures, demons had to be cast out of me.

Jesus bore my sin, sickness, curse, oppression, and depression by His death on the cross at Calvary. Hallelujah!

My husband and I have been married for over forty-seven years. By the grace of God, He has brought us this far and I know He will continue to work in our lives until Jesus comes. Jesus has truly changed both of us. I worship Him with all of my heart, and I give glory, honor, and praise to Him for all that He has done for us!

Chapter 1

EARLY CHILDHOOD AND BEING A JEHOVAH'S WITNESS

Each and every one of us is put on this earth for a reason. God has a purpose for each of our lives. This book contains my life story.

Since the very beginning, even in my mother's womb, not only did God have a plan for my life, but Satan did as well. It has been only through the grace of God that I am here today telling my story.

During my mother's eighth month of pregnancy, she fell in the bathtub and was rushed to the emergency room in hard labor. She almost delivered me in the elevator. She was quickly wheeled into the operating room and minutes later, I was born weighing 4 lbs. 12 oz. I was crippled with one clubfoot and one flat foot.

Several months later I underwent surgery and my feet were corrected. During this time I had to receive nine blood transfusions and I came so close to death. For many months I laid in my bed with casts on both legs, crying to be picked up and loved. As a year passed, even though the casts were removed, I had to crawl along the floor dragging my legs. The doctors said I would never walk, but my grandfather proved them wrong and taught me to walk at the age of two. I grew to be a healthy child.

Around the age of two, my mother and father divorced. Mother worked two jobs to support the family. I was the second child of three children. My grandmother lived with us for more than ten years, taking care of us while my mother worked. I was lonely as a young child because my mom was hardly around. When she was home, it felt like she favored the other children over me because my sister resembled her and my eldest brother looked like our dad. I felt left out of the family, but I was blessed with a special aunt who showed me affection during visits with her through the years.

We lived in a small, two-bedroom frame house in a poor area of Oklahoma City. My mother worked for Montgomery Wards Department Store during the day, and as a waitress at Harbor Lights, a dance hall, at night. It was really difficult for her to support us financially. She bought most of our clothes at the Goodwill and the Salvation Army, and my aunt would bring us clothing that her daughters had outgrown. We weren't particular about what we wore in those days, but I do know I hated to wear the long underwear and high top shoes in the wintertime when all the other girls in the neighborhood wore the latest fashions. But regardless of where the clothes came from, we appreciated them. They were new to us.

In those days of our youth, there wasn't much excitement or many things to do in the city, so my sister and I would improvise with our time. I remember one day as we went walking along the dirt road in front of our house, we found some cigarette butts on the ground. While no one was around to watch us, we picked up a few of them. We sneaked into the house, got some matches, slipped out the back door, ran to the chicken house in the backyard and lit up. I started puffing away. The more I puffed, the more I choked. The more I choked, the sicker I got. Before I knew it, I was throwing up. That special event ended my smoking career! Did we get into trouble when my mom came looking for us in the backyard and smelled the smoke! She was definitely a woman who did not believe in "sparing the rod"! Needless to say, we found better things to do with our time.

As far as church, we didn't go unless a neighbor invited us, which wasn't very often. Therefore, we didn't hear much about Jesus.

It was during this period of time that the Jehovah's Witnesses came into our lives. My aunt persuaded my mom to start having Bible studies in our home. Since there were few Kingdom Halls built in our area, the Witnesses held their meetings in different homes each week. The meetings were comparable to our cell groups in this day and time, but we didn't study the Bible much. We studied the literature written by the Watchtower and Tract Society.

Each week we studied the *Watchtower* and *Awake* magazines and we would have demonstrations with each other on how to go door-to-door witnessing. We memorized the speech that we would share at the door of a home. If it had not been for these practice sessions, I would not have known what to say about our beliefs. I did not fully understand all this teaching as a child growing up, but I accepted it because it was all that I had been taught.

Over the years I came to believe the Jehovah Witness' doctrine and believed all other religions were not of God. I firmly believed that we were the only ones who spoke the words of God's truth. I went wholeheartedly into the ministry of Jehovah's Witnesses, believing everything I was told.

I truly love Jehovah God with all of my heart, but I was not taught to love or to give praise to Jesus in any manner. After all, it was Jehovah God's plan of salvation, and Jesus did only what the Father told Him to do. I was told that we should appreciate what Jesus did for us on the "stake," but all worship was to go only to Jehovah God. In my heart there was unrest and confusion because I couldn't agree with this teaching or understand it. With this seed planted in my mind from around the age of eight, it grew and flourished in me.

As the years passed, I had this theology in my mind. I wouldn't receive or read any publications other than the Society's approved and published documents. Even though other Christian friends and relatives would tell me about Jesus, I wouldn't listen. I accepted all of the Jehovah Witness publications for preaching the "Good News." This was how we got the "meat" of God's Word to help us grow.

The Jehovah Witnesses believe that Jehovah God's active force – the Holy Spirit – was poured upon all "Brothers" in Bethel, New York, for producing all of their literature, including their Bible called *New World Translation of the Holy Scriptures*. Without studying the Bible for myself to see if this was indeed the truth, I just remained ignorant to the real truth and believed only the things I was told. We were told we had boldness but that we didn't have the Holy Spirit to help us witness or to give us understanding. This teaching is definitely not scriptural according to God's Holy Bible.

There are many other Bible translations, such as the *King James, New International Version,* and the *New American Standard,* which state in Acts 2:16-18:

> **"But this is what was spoken by the prophet Joel: 'And it shall come to pass in the last days, says God, that I will pour out of My Spirit on all flesh; your sons and your daughters shall prophesy, your young men shall see visions, your old men shall dream dreams.**
>
> **"'And on My menservants and on My maidservants I will pour out My Spirit in those days . . . .'"**
>
> NKJV

God says, "In the last days (which many theologians agree we are living in right now), My Spirit will be poured out on all flesh!" That means **me**, too! Plus, when we receive Jesus as our Lord and Savior, the Person of the Holy Spirit comes to live in our hearts. God says the Holy Spirit will lead us and guide us into all truth.

> **"However, when He, the Spirit of truth, has come, He will guide you into all truth; for He will not speak on His own authority, but whatever He hears He will speak; and He will tell you things to come.**

"He will glorify Me, for He will take of what is Mine and declare it to you."

John 16:13-14 NKJV

I didn't know at that time that I needed this knowledge to help me learn and understand the Word of God. When we went to the Kingdom Hall, during the Watchtower and Awake study we were expected to answer questions from the publications only. We were not to quote scriptures from the Bible as a reference because the answers were already given by the Society which they believed were straight from Jehovah God, due to the fact that they believed and taught that the Society was the only one that had the Holy Spirit and heard from God.

Jesus said in John 14:26, **"But the Comforter, which is the Holy Ghost, whom the Father will send in my name, he shall teach you all things, and bring all things to your remembrance, whatsoever I have said unto you."** This tells me that the Holy Spirit will speak to <u>you</u> and <u>me</u> because God is no respecter of persons!

At this point, many questions started arising in my mind. One of my questions was, "Why won't they accept the answers from their own Bible?" My aunt was laughed at many times during the meetings because she offered different scriptural answers from the Bible, rather than from the publications. She was publicly cautioned to give only the answers that the Watchtower provided. Even in their midst, she spoke up for the truth of God's Word.

Many times when I went to visit my aunt, she had been studying the *King James Version* of the Bible. She watched Reverend Billy Graham on television many times and agreed with the plan of salvation through Jesus Christ, but she did not believe in a literal hell for people.

Even though the Bible clearly speaks of hell, even more than heaven, let's examine the Word of God on this subject. Matthew 18:8-9 NKJV states:

If your hand or foot causes you to sin, cut it off and cast it from you. It is better for you to enter into life lame or maimed, rather than having two hands or two feet, to be cast into the everlasting fire.

And if your eye causes you to sin, pluck it out and cast it from you. It is better for you to enter into life with one eye, rather than having two eyes, to be cast into hell fire.

This is only two verses of scripture that prove that hell does exist and people will go there even though this is not God's plan for man. John 3:16 says, **"For God so loved the world, that he gave his only begotten Son, that whosoever believeth in him should not perish, but have everlasting life."** My aunt remained steadfast in her faith in the doctrine of Jehovah Witnesses.

A few years went by and we remained in the Kingdom work, going house to house with the *Watchtower* and *Awake* magazines. Looking back at the thirty-three years of being a Jehovah's Witness, never did I use their Bible as a reference to support or validate their doctrine as truth while witnessing. If I had used their Bible to substantiate the claims I was making, I would have misinterpreted God's written Word.

I thank God that when I go door-to-door witnessing as a born-again Christian, I don't have to worry about what I am going to say. God says when I open my mouth to share the gospel of the Lord Jesus Christ, He will fill it with His words. The Holy Spirit will speak through me what He wants me to say. How about that?

The Holy Spirit led me to meditate on His Word in the book of Jeremiah, chapter 1, verses 4-10:

Then the word of the LORD came unto me, saying,

Before I formed thee in the belly I knew thee; and before thou camest forth out of the womb I

sanctified thee, and I ordained thee a prophet unto the nations.

Then said I, Ah, Lord God! behold, I cannot speak: for I am a child.

But the LORD said unto me, Say not, I am a child: for thou shalt go to all that I shall send thee, and whatsoever I command thee thou shalt speak.

Be not afraid of their faces: for I am with thee to deliver thee, saith the LORD.

Then the LORD put forth his hand, and touched my mouth. And the LORD said unto me, Behold, I have put my words in thy mouth.

See, I have this day set thee over the nations and over the kingdoms, to root out, and to pull down, and to destroy, and to throw down, to build, and to plant.

I don't have to worry about memorizing a presentation to the public because God has prepared me. God has put it into my heart to study His Word. Second Timothy 2:15 says, **"Study to shew thyself approved unto God, a workman that needeth not to be ashamed, rightly dividing the word of truth."** As I do this every day, then God brings the Word out of me when it is needed. The Word of God is already in my heart. What a joy it is to serve the True and Living God. There is such an abundance of joy when the Holy Spirit moves through me and gives me the words to speak. The Bible says in Proverbs 15:23, **"A man hath joy by the answer of his mouth: and a word spoken in due season, how good is it!"**

As a Jehovah Witness, we were supposed to work in the field service sixty hours a month to be called "active." But due to my mother's occupations, we were not as consistent as we should have been; therefore, the elders of the Kingdom Hall put us as "inactive." I'm so glad now that I don't have to keep a record of my time spent serving the Lord, because He already knows.

Chapter 2

COUNTRY LIVING AND NEW STEPFATHER

As time passed, my mother remarried and we moved to the country outside of McLoud, Oklahoma. I really enjoyed living in the country, but I quickly learned one thing about country living. Chores!

People always think they have to have a cow around the house to give fresh milk and good ole bright yellow churned butter. Naturally, who got picked to milk the cow? You guessed right! Me! I think I got more milk on my shoes and on the cow's hoofs than I did in the bucket! Plus, I put those chains around her hoofs so close to keep her from putting her foot in the bucket that if you were to look at her, you would think she was standing on one foot! She was a gentle ole cow to put up with me.

These chores needed to be done before the school bus came, because my mom had to leave early to go to work. In time, I got the hang of it and it wasn't so bad. My brother fed the pigs because he raised them for school projects and my sister helped feed the chickens and turkeys. Every night those twelve spoiled turkeys would line up on top of the gate leading to the chicken yard, and one by one we had to lift them off and carry them into the chicken house! And did we have turkey for Thanksgiving? No! They were pets!

We had a special rooster that loved to chase my sister and me as we went back and forth from the house to the outhouse (we had no indoor bathroom). It was pretty far away so we usually waited for each other so we wouldn't have to go alone. We knew that he would always be around to frighten us, so we would hold each other's hands and run like the dickens.

One evening we made it safely to the outhouse and when we were ready to leave, we peeked outside the door to see if the rooster was near. He was nowhere in sight. I said, "All right, the coast is clear. Let's get out of here!" We opened the door and took off running as fast as we could, but before we got halfway to the house, the ole rooster was right behind us! He started jumping at our feet, trying to flog us. We screamed and cried and tried to shoo him away, but to no avail. We had to maneuver ourselves back to the house the best we could. Finally, we reached the porch without physical injury, but we were so frightened. We told our mom what happened and she boldly replied, "That rooster will not hurt you if you show it you are not afraid. Look, I'll show you that it won't hurt anyone."

So mom went outside, down the trail to the outhouse, and here came the "harmless" rooster. A few minutes later, Mom came back into the house with the back of her legs and ankles scratched and bleeding. Not muttering a word, she boldly marched into the living room, took the rifle off of the gun rack above the fireplace, and went outside. I tell you, she had determination in her eyes and not a lick of fear in her bones! She found that "harmless" rooster, cocked that rifle, aimed, and shot its head off! What a relief! We were thrilled and happy that we didn't have to be afraid anymore.

On the twenty acres on which we lived, there was a spring-fed creek. Sometimes it would get about six feet deep and we would all go swimming. One afternoon, a girlfriend of mine from school wanted me to teach her how to swim. That was fine with me because when we lived in Oklahoma City, I had learned to swim at the YWCA. So we both went into the water and eventually it came up to our necks.

Suddenly, she panicked and jumped onto me, pushing my entire body underwater. She was so terrified, she literally held me under the water! I didn't know what to do. I thought, *Oh, God, I'm going to drown! What can I do?* A strong voice that I don't recall ever hearing before said to me, "Take her by the waist and shove her toward the embankment as hard as you can!" I obeyed what the voice told me to do.

As I shoved her loose from me, she fell into shallow water against the bank and I immediately came up out of the water, choking and spitting up water. She said she was sorry that she had gotten so scared. I wasn't angry with her, but I do thank God that He answered my prayer. I didn't know at the time that it was the Holy Spirit who spoke to me and saved my life. I had never been taught that God speaks to us.

Our lives seemed to change after my mom's second marriage. Even though my stepfather wasn't a Jehovah Witness, he would appease Mom by attending some of the services at the Kingdom Hall. Only having an eighth grade education, everyone called him a "Jack of all trades." It seemed he was capable of doing anything, and he was willing to help others at anytime. He was an intelligent man and he worked the same job as a welder for almost thirty years.

Right away, he and my mom bought an old house and moved it thirty miles down the highway. The house being moved would not go under a bridge because of its height. So right there on the highway, they had to get a construction team to cut off the roof of the house to move it farther. What a hassle! Finally, days later, they got it moved and placed on the acreage. It took years of hard work to make it livable. It was so cold during the winter that we closed off many rooms to keep warm. All five of us lived in one or two rooms. This is what you call "togetherness"! Years later, my stepfather built an upstairs, he put in indoor plumbing and a beautiful rock fireplace which really helped in the wintertime.

One day, Mom and I came home from shopping in town and my stepfather was lying on the hearth passed out drunk. Alcohol had become his worst problem and in later years, his health deteriorated. His drinking made it difficult sometimes to live in the house because there was so much arguing and cursing between my parents when he was drunk. There seemed to be no lasting peace in our home. I couldn't understand why they were like that because at the Kingdom Hall they acted so different, so friendly and kind to everyone, but at home, behind closed doors, it was another story.

I used to walk one-fourth of a mile to my girlfriend's house to visit with her. I noticed her parents and her brothers. Even though her parents were elderly, something was different about them. There was such a peace in their lives. As her mother sat in a chair, her husband squatted beside her and held her hand! They talked so quietly and gently to each other, and I know it wasn't just because I was there. This was their lifestyle!

They farmed a blackberry patch that they rented, and each year during blackberry season, we would be there at the crack of dawn until sunset picking baskets of blackberries for six cents a basket. I never heard a cross word coming from the neighbors all the years we lived near them. Later, I found out that they were Christians. I thought we were too! So what were we missing? **JESUS!**

My parents were like two different people – godly in the Kingdom Hall and like the devil at home. There were always arguments over not enough money to pay bills, but my stepfather always managed to get a bottle of whiskey. When my mom would find the bottle hidden away, she would pour it down the drain. He quickly went a few miles down the road and got another one on credit.

After twenty-three years of marriage, he was eventually hospitalized with cancer of the liver and lung disease. He was a heavy smoker too. After many months of suffering, at the age of fifty-three and weighing only about 70 pounds, he passed away. Before he died, we were able to visit with him in the hospital. He told many of the family members how sorry he was for the life he had lived and asked for forgiveness. We all loved him regardless of his ways, and we did forgive him. It was there in the hospital that he repented of all his sins and asked Jesus to come into his heart and save him, accepting Christ as his Lord and Savior. One of his relatives was a Baptist preacher who prayed with him. At that time, I had no knowledge of how to pray that prayer with him.

Looking back over the past, I can remember seeing an open Bible on our bathroom counter after he would leave the room.

We always made fun of him because he always stayed so long. He was reading! I know now that, although he didn't seem to be a religious man, he still read the Word of God and had faith to believe in Jesus for his salvation regardless of the problems he had in his life that he could not overcome by himself.

Second Peter 3:9 says, **"The Lord is not slack concerning his promise, as some men count slackness; but is longsuffering to usward, not willing that any should perish, but that all should come to repentance."**

Chapter 3

I Met My Adorable Husband To Be

During my teen years, my brother, at the age of seventeen, joined the Army and went to Fort Bliss, Texas, for basic training. It was while he was in El Paso at the Army base that my brother went to the PX and there he met Oscar Hernandez, a young Hispanic who was working there. My brother showed him my school picture and asked if he wanted to write to me. Needless to say, we started writing to each other as pen pals. I was fifteen years old at the time.

Several months later, my stepfather (before his death) decided he would drive the family to El Paso to see my brother at the base. It was then that I got to meet Oscar and his family for the first time. When we walked into the PX, my cousin, who came on the trip with us, started looking for him. She was just as excited about meeting him as I was. I only had a picture to go by.

Suddenly, a young man came from around the corner and I asked, "Are you Oscar Hernandez?" He laughed and said, "No, he's in the other room." So he called out for him and said, "Oscar, there is a cute young girl here to see you." Immediately, he came with a big grin on his face. He knew beforehand that we were coming to meet him. I reached out to shake his hand and I think he held my hand for at least ten minutes, smiling and staring at me with those big brown eyes until I turned completely red! I felt so embarrassed. He was so cute and quiet.

Finally, Mom came over to us and started a conversation with him and the tension lifted. We met his parents that night, and the next day Oscar took us on a tour to Juarez, Mexico. Oscar bought me a beautiful necklace set and we took home several souvenirs. A couple of days later, after seeing my brother, we went back home. It was really a neat trip. Oscar and I continued to correspond through letters as months passed.

Oscar visited my home in Oklahoma a couple of times before he joined the Air Force. A few months later, after basic training, he visited with us once again before he was flown to Japan for a two-year tour of duty. Oscar bought me a beautiful engagement ring before he left, but I hesitated to accept that commitment because I was only sixteen and I didn't really know him that well just by corresponding with him those few months. But he wouldn't take "no" for an answer, and he left the ring so I could think about it.

Almost two years passed and we still continued to write to each other during that time. I was still uncertain concerning the engagement, but I had very few dates during my high school years. My mom was quite strict about my dating. I believe most of it was because of her religious background.

Chapter 4

HIGH SCHOOL YEARS

During those high school days, I was well liked and I received many honors. I was chosen Spring Festival Queen, Basketball Queen Runner-up, and senior year president of the Future Homemakers of America. I received a four-year letter jacket in basketball, and I believe that was for being the best "benchwarmer" on the team! Either we were twenty points ahead or twenty points behind when I got to play! Did I care? No, I got to go right along with the team even to State one year. My sister was on the main string. She was skinny and little and could run like the wind. In practice, the coach made me chase her down! But I was a really good cheerleader and bench-warmer! It didn't matter. I was there with the best of them.

In 1956, my junior year, I was chosen by the American Legion Auxiliary to go to Girls' State to learn about Oklahoma Government at USAO College in Chickasha, Oklahoma. I spent a week there, along with other girls from across the state. I was nominated State Representative Number 6. I thought to myself, *What could I do for Oklahoma while I am in office?* I was given a long list of offices from which to make my selection. My certificate read:

Oklahoma Girls' State 1956 American Legion Auxiliary. This is to certify that Emma Lou Losawyer [my maiden name] **of the City of Rice, County of Brown, of Oklahoma Girls' State held at the Oklahoma College for Women, Chickasha, Oklahoma, June 2-9, 1956, has conducted herself with honor and credit as a citizen and has fulfilled to the best of her ability all assignments given her. Her sponsor or sponsors, who made possible her participation as a leader in this**

practical application of the American principles of Government, have every right to expect of her a continuation of unselfish leadership in affairs of education and government in her city, her county, and her state.

Special Honors and Offices in Girls' State.

Member, State Party Committee – State Representative, Chairman of the Penal and Eleemosynary Committee in the House.

Signed, Lois Brown, Department President and LeNora Biggert, Girls' State Director.

I chose to learn about the penal (prison) system and to work in it. Little did I know, God had instilled this in my heart. Now, forty years later, I am an ordained minister of the Lord Jesus Christ.

For the past fourteen years, I have been ministering in the prisons in Oklahoma, Texas, and Mexico. The uniqueness of this is that in 1956 I wasn't even a Christian and I had no clue why I chose such a career. But now I know. God had a plan for me in this area and in His timing, it would come to pass.

I held a part-time job after school working at a grocery store as a cashier. One evening after school, a classmate came into the store with her boyfriend and his brother. She came over to me and said her friend thought I was cute and he wanted to know if I could go to a movie with them in another little town not far from there. I told her that I needed to get permission from my mother before I would do that, so after work they followed me home.

After arriving home, I asked Mom if I could go on this blind date. Usually, my mom without question would say "no"! I told her that I did not know him, but I had no reason not to trust them because I went to school with the girl every day and it was her friend's brother. Without hesitation or asking any questions about the young men, she said "yes" much to my surprise. Oh, if only I had hindsight before going with these young people. If I had known then what I know now, what pain and suffering I could have been spared. "How?" you might ask. If only I had known how to listen to the voice of the Holy Spirit to know this was not a good decision. I didn't have such teaching, so I couldn't recognize any warnings. Besides, the young man seemed nice enough.

As we drove down the highway to go to the theater in the next town, I soon realized we were not going in the direction we were supposed to be going. I commented on this as I was led to believe that we were going to a movie. The driver replied that they had decided not to go to a movie, but to go down a country road to park for a while.

Several miles down the highway, he turned off onto a dirt road and parked. The other young man and my classmate began to take the backseat out of the car. I asked, "What are you doing?" The girl replied that they were just going to sit down on the side of the road for a while. The young man I was with drove about a half mile farther down the road and parked. Then, he put his arm around me and with the other hand slipped it into my blouse and started fondling me. This was a whole new experience for me, and at the age of sixteen I wasn't ready for such an adventure. So I grabbed his arm and told him not to do that! Of course, this angered him and he said if I didn't let him do what he wanted, I had to get out of the car. My first choice was, get out of the car! So since I didn't want him to continue with his maneuver, he leaned over me, opened the car door, and proceeded to push me out of the car.

My thoughts raged within me as I fell on the ground. *This is not good! Something is wrong here!* I jumped to my feet, and not knowing what to do, I was so scared, I ran as fast and as far as my feet could take me. I screamed and screamed, but there was no one to help me. He caught up with me, grabbed me by the throat, and said, "If you scream any more, I'll kill you!"

Then, he dragged me back to the car with his hands still on my throat. I was so scared and shaking all over. He shoved me down into the front seat, lifted my skirt, and began to rape me. I kept screaming and crying, but he just kept hurting me and kept his hand at my throat during the entire ordeal. Finally, he quit.

As he pulled away from me, he saw by his headlights that he had raped a virgin. Blood was all over him. Then, he came to the driver's side of the car and told me that he was sorry for what he had done and asked me to forgive him. Then, he cried out to God, "Forgive me for what I have just done to this girl!" Again, he asked me to forgive him, and I said, "I forgive you." I don't know if he was really sorry for his actions, only the Lord knows. He told me not to tell anyone what had happened, but the next day I told my classmate, and she apologized for him because she didn't know him either. Had she known his character, she would not have invited me, she said. But I was never the same after that trauma.

Even though apologies came forth, I still did not know what I had done to deserve this horrible treatment. It's like every evil spirit in hell came into me. Rejection, abuse, guilt, oppression, depression, you name it. I felt like it was my entire fault because I went with someone I didn't know. I felt dirty and betrayed.

I was afraid to tell my mother, but a few days later she asked me why I was so quiet. Then, I broke down crying, telling her what had happened to me. My mother was angry with me. From that day on I lost her trust. She accused me of wanting to do bad things with other young men who called me from school for a date. Those evil thoughts never entered my mind. I hated the thought of being around boys from that time on. I thought, *How did I forgive that mean, cruel, degrading young man of his maliciousness?* I didn't know how. Only by the grace of God could a person do that. With my mom's new attitude toward me, I hated living at home. I felt such rejection and emptiness. I wanted to run away and never come back.

Months later while visiting my aunt, I told her what happened to me. She said, "Emma, did you scream?" I told her,

"Yes, several times, loud and clear, but there was no one to help me!" She then put her arms around me and said, "Emma, in the Bible God says in Deuteronomy 22:25-27 that if a virgin is in a pasture and a man comes and forces her and defiles her, if she screams and there is no one to help her, it is not her fault. God does not hold her responsible" (my aunt's interpretation). Oh, how those words of Scripture comforted me since I felt so much guilt from what had happened. I also blamed my mother for allowing me to go out with the young man without meeting him, and later showing no concern, mercy, or even pity for what had happened to me . I appreciated my aunt for sharing the Word of God with me because it was the only thing that gave me real peace. Then, I felt like a heavy burden I was carrying was lifted off of my shoulders.

I cried unto the Lord and made a vow to Him. If He would help me through the trauma without me obtaining any disease or getting pregnant, I would serve Him the rest of my life, and I meant it. As a result of this incident, and now being a born-again Christian and studying the Word of God, I have been emotionally healed by the power of God's love, mercy, and grace. I am now able to face men and any offenders without prejudice in many prisons and places God sends me to preach the gospel of the Lord Jesus Christ. I can now minister to men and women who have also been raped, molested, and abused because of what I have gone through in my life.

I learned how to forgive those who hurt me, including my own mother. Jesus says in Matthew 6:14-15 NKJV, **"For if you forgive men their trespasses, your heavenly Father will also forgive you. But if you do not forgive men their trespasses, neither will your Father forgive your trespasses."** In Mark 11:25-26 NKJV Jesus says, **"And whenever you stand praying, if you have anything against anyone, forgive him, that your Father in heaven may also forgive you your trespasses. But if you do not forgive, neither will your Father in heaven forgive your trespasses."** There are no options to this rule. Jesus said it and He meant what He said.

I read the beatitudes in Matthew 5:1-12 regularly. In verses 11-12 NKJV, Jesus said, **"Blessed are you when they revile and persecute you, and say all kinds of evil against you falsely for My sake. Rejoice and be exceedingly glad, for great is your reward in heaven, for so they <u>persecuted</u> the prophets who were before you."** Now I have peace. No more guilt or condemnation.

Chapter 5

MARRIAGE TO OSCAR

Regardless of what had happened in my life, I continued living with my parents and graduated in 1957 with honors. Afterwards I went to work at Sylvania in Shawnee, Oklahoma. I continued writing letters to Oscar and some pen pals, which lifted me up.

In February 1958, after Oscar's tour of duty in Japan, he came to Oklahoma after visiting with his mom in Texas. We decided to get married and it had to be within a week due to his reassignment to Bossier City, Louisiana.

So first things first. We needed to get the blood test. The doctor, after drawing the blood samples, advised us not to get married. Oscar was told he had a rare blood type and I was RH negative. The doctor stated that our blood would not be compatible when it came to having children. He stated that the antibodies in my blood would kill the antibodies in the blood of our babies if they were not RH negative. He also said that it would cause our babies to be mentally retarded, stillborn, missing limbs, or cause me to miscarry. Now, wasn't that a sweet note to sing to you with your hopes of getting married? (To jump ahead of my story, we did get married and I did have two miscarriages, but we were still blessed with five other beautiful, healthy, normal children.)

We took the doctor's advice with a grain of salt and continued on to our next destination. We needed to get the approval from the chaplain at Tinker Air Force Base in Oklahoma to get married. Much to our surprise, as we talked with him, he advised us not to get married because of our religious backgrounds. Oscar was raised Catholic, and I was still a Jehovah Witness. The chaplain believed that there would not be a close spiritual relationship between us or with God. "There is no bridge between you," he stated. So a little bit of discouragement set in, but we didn't give up!

We went back to my house and told my mother what had transpired during the two visits to the doctor and the chaplain. She advised us to go to the Kingdom Hall and ask one of the elders if he would marry us. This we did and he also said, "No." He said that I would be marrying an unbeliever and the Word of God says not to become unevenly yoked with unbelievers. So three times in the same day by three different people at different times, we were told, "Don't get married!" Did we listen? Of course not!

The following day we went and got our marriage license. Three days later on February 18, 1958, my brother and sister-in-law rode with us to the Justice of the Peace outside of Oklahoma City in a small, run-down building. We sat and pondered, *Do we really want to do this?* We were so quiet about this dramatic decision that my sister-in-law laughed at us, and said, "Well, you can't back out now!" Did we get cold feet at the last minute? Thoughts went through my mind, *Do I want to get married, or do I want to continue living in my dysfunctional family?* I thought surely marriage to this handsome, young, twenty-year-old man couldn't be any worse than what I had to live with. So without any more hesitation, we decided to go ahead with the marriage plans.

Another thought I'm having right now after forty-seven years have passed and being a Christian, is due to our hesitation, could it have been that the Holy Spirit of God was trying to talk to us, and say, "Wait, Emma. I have a better plan for you"? Perhaps it wasn't the right timing. Nevertheless, we married and are still married to this day, forty-seven years later. Praise the Lord! This just shows me if we don't follow God's perfect plan the first time, He'll make another one and turn the old one around for good, so we can give Him glory!

Now, back to the story. We went into the building and met the Justice of the Peace. As we stood in front of him, he had us sign the marriage certificate. Then, he told us to hold hands with each other, as he said, "Oscar, do you take this woman, Emma Lou Losawyer, to be your lawful wedded wife?" He replied, "I do." Then turning to me, he said, "Emma Lou Losawyer, do you take Oscar Hernandez to be your lawful wedded husband?" I replied, "I do." He then pronounced us man and wife. "That will be $10.00, please!"

I stood there in awe thinking there should have been more to this ceremony. This certainly wasn't anything like I had seen on TV! Here I was wearing a beautiful wedding gown that my neighbor and I made, and Oscar wearing a nice suit. Something was missing. It felt so empty and lifeless because I heard no other confessions of commitment or vows to each other or to God that would have consecrated our marriage. I turned to look at the Justice of the Peace, and with an expression of, "Is this all there is to it?" he replied without me saying another word, "Oh, you wanted more?" "Well, yes," I replied. He led us to repeat a few more words to each other, which made the ceremony sound more complete.

Later that evening, my mother held a surprise reception for us at our home. Afterwards, our friends and relatives got in separate cars to take us to Shawnee, twelve miles away. I was taken in one car and Oscar in another. When we arrived at the edge of town, all of the cars and trucks that were with us stopped in the middle of the street and unloaded a wheelbarrow from one of the trucks. I was told to get in it and Oscar had to push me down Main Street for three blocks! Can't you just imagine this? Me wearing a beautiful wedding dress sitting in the middle of a wheelbarrow? (I'm sure glad he didn't dump me out!") Other people were honking their horns, waving their hands, and wishing us well. Even though it was bitter cold, it was a very memorable time I won't forget.

After the fun was over, everyone departed for their homes. We were taken together back to my home to pick up our car that we had saved money for before we got married. Then, we left for Oklahoma City. Before reaching the city limits and while going across some railroad tracks, our car stalled. This was a scary situation! It was so late at night, hardly anyone was around, but suddenly, a car came by and we were able to flag the driver down. The nice gentleman helped us push the car off of the tracks. It still took us several hours to get a mechanic to come and help us at that hour. But finally, just before midnight, we made it to a motel in the city. What a dramatic beginning we had to our marriage!

The following day, we went to my home to collect my personal belongings and gifts, and then we left for Louisiana. After we arrived in Bossier City, Louisiana, we found an apartment near the base and moved in. A person would think that immediately after you had gotten married that your love for each other would begin growing deeper and stronger as time went by. Just the opposite happened in our case. As weeks and months passed, anger, jealously, and strife entered our relationship. It seemed like a total turnaround.

In all the letters I had received from Oscar over the years we corresponded, there were deep expressions of love. It was a love that I thought was genuine, but later it seemed to be only a disguise for the loneliness and emptiness he felt while overseas. Because of trauma in my own life, I couldn't relate to him as a wife as I should have. I needed an inner healing and a feeling of acceptance. Little did I know that this healing could only come from God Himself.

Sometimes it takes time to heal, and at other times, the healing is instantaneous. God is the only One who can reach deep down into your heart and deliver you from the oppression of mental or physical abuse. The healing I needed could not come from my husband because he didn't have an understanding of what rape victims go through. During the `50s, no one ever spoke of being raped. It was hidden and never talked about. I was told not to share my past with my husband so I concealed it as long as I could. But before the first year of marriage was up, one night I was forced to reveal to him what had happened to me as a teenager. That revelation hurt my husband very much and it caused him to have mistrust for me from then on. This was one area in our life that we had to work on, and it was a long, hard road.

Chapter 6

CURSE OF WITCHCRAFT

In this chapter, I will share some graphic statements of demonic activity that actually happened to me. In later years, it attacked my family. This activity lasted for twenty-one years.

Right now, in the name of Jesus Christ of Nazareth, I come against any spirit of fear that would try to enter into the mind of anyone reading this book. By the authority, power, name, and the blood of Jesus, I rebuke you, Satan, and command you to leave the premises of these people and not come back.

This chapter is intended to enlighten others to the demonic strongholds Satan can have on a person if there is no knowledge of demonic activity. I am compelled to write this because of the rise of interest in the occult, witchcraft, and other evil things that Satan subtly tries to bring into our society. In libraries and schools today, there are books for children that teach how to cast spells of witchcraft on others. People believe they can receive supernatural power from these teachings. If so, this power does not come from Jesus!

In many stores, there are games and videos that the young and innocent can buy for what some would think are entertainment. Fantasy, they call it. No harm to it, but people will spend hours watching the supernatural powers of the evil one on television, then wonder why they can't sleep at night because of fear! Then, there are games on the computer that can send the same messages to you and even though the children are probably not old enough to understand it is evil, they will indulge in these games until something starts happening in their lives.

What are some of the symptoms that occur? Unexplained sickness or pain, and even if you go to a doctor, there wouldn't be a diagnosis of anything wrong with you. This is just an example of what can happen. There is more to come because Satan won't stop there. In the night, there will be nightmares just like I went through. Believe me, you don't want to go there! If you believe it's all fun and games, after you read this true story, you can decide for yourself.

I know in my heart it is no game! Satan doesn't play games! He is out for your eternal soul to be damned with him! Read the back of the Bible, and you'll find out that he's a loser and he wants you with him, just like he was after me and my family. From what I understand, I am still on Satan's most wanted list! But the Bible says, **"If God be for us, who can be against us?"** (Romans 8:31). What happened to me and my family can happen to you! I was a victim of someone's game, jealousy, or hatred. Only the Lord knows!

The Ouija Board – another game? You bring in the supernatural, and it is not the Holy Spirit speaking to you through the moving of the mouse to the letters which form words. In this way, you invite the devil into your house. I played with this board a few times trying to get answers for my dilemma, but I was unsuccessful in any attempts to get an answer that would help me, so I quit playing with it.

Also, once the demons are in your house, they're not easy to get rid of. You might just say they came with their suitcases and have decided to stay awhile since they were invited in. They will by no means be ready to leave unless you know who you are in Christ Jesus and boot them out by the power of God. There is no other way out! They will set up residence, especially if you don't know Jesus as your Lord and Savior, and are covered by His precious blood! You can say, "I'll just repent, get rid of the books, objects, etc., and all will be well...."

Scripture is very clear on this subject. In Matthew 12:43-45 NKJV Jesus states:

"When an unclean spirit goes out of a man, he goes through dry places, seeking rest, and finds none.

"Then he says, 'I will return to my house from which I came.' And when he comes, he finds it empty, swept, and put in order.

"Then he goes and takes with him seven other spirits more wicked than himself, and they enter and dwell there; and the last state of that man is worse than the first. So shall it also be with this wicked generation."

I believe this is referring to a person more so than to a house. When a man, woman, or child receives deliverance from demonic possession, unless he receives Jesus as Lord and Savior and gets the Word of God in his heart, then the demons will come back as the Scripture states so clearly. It's true in a literal house. We call them "haunted houses." Unless someone takes authority over them in the name of Jesus Christ of Nazareth, and has that power and the anointing to do so, they won't leave.

What can you do if you are in this situation? James 4:6-8 NKJV says, **"But He gives more grace. Therefore He says: 'God resists the proud, but gives grace to the humble.' Therefore submit to God. Resist the devil and he will flee from you. Draw near to God and He will draw near to you. . . ."** When you are totally submitted to God, the Holy Spirit will reveal to you what you should do or not do to keep you on the path of righteousness. You won't walk in fear as I did because I did not know God's Word nor had I put it in my heart.

Once a year, in the United States we celebrate Halloween. A child wants to be a witch or a warlock. It's cute and everybody is doing it! What's the harm? God, in His Word, says to stay away from even the appearance of evil. In the Old Testament, witches were put to death, and they were an abomination to the Lord. Scripture calls them "forbidden pagan practices." Deuteronomy 18:9-14 says:

When thou art come into the land which the LORD thy God giveth thee, thou shalt not learn to do after the abominations of those nations.

There shall not be found among you any one that maketh his son or his daughter to pass through the fire, or that useth divination, or an observer of times, or an enchanter, or a witch,

Or a charmer, or a consulter with familiar spirits, or a wizard, or a necromancer.

For all that do these things are an abomination unto the LORD: and because of these abominations the LORD thy God doth drive them out from before thee.

Thou shalt be perfect with the LORD thy God.

For these nations, which thou shalt possess, hearkened unto observers of times, and unto diviners: but as for thee, the LORD thy God hath not suffered thee so to do.

You may say, "That is in the Old Testament. We're not under the Law anymore!" But, don't forget. Jesus came to fulfill the Law, not to abolish it! Galatians 5:19-21 in the New Testament says:

Now the works of the flesh are manifest, which are these; Adultery, fornication, uncleanness, lasciviousness,

Idolatry, witchcraft, hatred, variance, emulations, wrath, strife, seditions, heresies,

Envyings, murders, drunkenness, revellings, and such like: of the which I tell you before, as I have also told you in time past, that they which do such things shall not inherit the kingdom of God.

Am I making myself clear? I want to warn people, and tell them that the devil is as real as God, and he has a plan for your life, which is not good! In John 10:10 Jesus says, **"The thief cometh not, but for to steal, and to kill, and to destroy: I am come that they might have life, and that they might**

have it more abundantly." The Holy Spirit, will reveal Truth to you. It's up to you as to what you will do with it. And the story goes on . . .

As months passed, I became pregnant with our first daughter. I had morning sickness for what seemed like forever. It hindered me from keeping house "white glove clean" as some military men expect of their wives. So to keep things more interesting, I now believe Satan unveiled a little more of his plan to destroy my husband and me.

At night, I began to hear noises. It sounded like the footsteps of someone walking back and forth in the living room. I woke my husband and told him that I thought a burglar was in the house. Immediately he got up and took the rifle out of the closet. He went into the living room, peered around doors, and found no one was there! So he came back to bed and said, "You must have been dreaming. There is no one there and the doors are locked." He lay down and quickly fell asleep.

A few minutes later, the noise returned, but this time it was much louder. It sounded like chains were being dragged across the floor. Scared and shaking, I shook Oscar and told him what I was hearing. Again, he got up believing what I had said. He stood quietly in the room and listened. He heard nothing nor saw anything, so he came back and got into bed. Again he said to me, "Go back to sleep. You have to be dreaming."

Night after night and year after year, this torment continued. All I could do was lie in bed and cry. I screamed, shook, trembled, and pulled the covers over my head, but nothing helped. One night I pulled the covers over my head so I wouldn't see anything. I laid there and didn't move an inch. I was sweating from tremendous fear of what was going to happen next. Suddenly, the covers started being drawn from my body, from the top of my head to my feet from the end of the bed. What should I do? I didn't see anyone or anything in our room, but something supernatural was terrifying me! What would any sensible person do? I pulled the covers right back over my head!

Believe it or not, we (whoever or whatever was at the end of my bed) had a tug-of-war going on in my bedroom over my covers! Eventually, I gave up and the covers ended up at the end of my feet! My husband wasn't even aware that anything was going on! He slept through the whole thing. This was just one incident that happened to me.

There were so many different occurrences that happened to me, it wasn't even funny. For many years, my husband just lay quietly and peaceably beside me sleeping away the night. I was always awakened by a cold feeling or a chilling presence that came over my whole body. As I turned my head, there in front of me, I could see with my natural eyes a supernatural being. I do not know to this day why my eyes were opened to see the evil of the supernatural. But I thank God every day that I do not see those spirits of evil anymore.

Anyway, some people may refer to them as spirits, ghosts, demons, or apparitions. But I don't care about their definitions because they brought me so much fear and torment that I felt like it came from the pit of hell.

This particular time, the thing resembled a person. It knelt beside my bed with the most horrifying face I had ever seen. His eyes glowed in different colors of red and gold, but oh, so terrifying, staring at me right in the face. All I could do was turn away and scream. Of course, Oscar woke up and asked me what was wrong. As I turned back around to show him what I saw, it was gone! He didn't see anything. He couldn't understand why I was the only one having all these "nightmares," as he called them.

It was so unbelievable that as my husband would lie back down to go to sleep, he slept so peaceably. I just laid there beside him, trembling with fear! I tried to convince myself that it was nothing to worry about, and perhaps I was just dreaming or having a nightmare, like my husband said. I thought maybe if I would think on other things, it would go away. But as time passed, that wasn't the answer.

The occurrences happened more frequently and became more tormenting. I lived nearly every night in constant fear of the unknown. Was I going crazy? Was this just my imagination playing tricks on me? I tried to figure out in my mind what could be happening.

When I was a little girl, my brother used to sleep in our bedroom (my sister and I shared the same bed), because our house had only two bedrooms. During the night sometimes, just for kicks, he would say to me, "Emma, look over at the closet. Someone is in there, and he wants to get you!" Or, "Someone is looking at you through the window!" And, if that wasn't enough or if that didn't make his night, he quietly crawled out of his bed, spread out his fingers, and screeched AAAAHHHH at me and ran back and jumped into his bed laughing, with me laying there in bed screaming and crying. My mom ran into the room and asked what was going on, and as I told her what had happened, she just scolded my brother and told me to go back to sleep. I was so shook up, it wasn't that easy to go back to sleep!

Looking back on those days, I don't believe he intentionally tried to hurt me; he was just having fun, but at my expense. But I did wonder if those earlier experiences had any bearing on what had been happening to me. I couldn't understand why it wasn't happening to my husband. When he wakes up, the voices quit speaking; noises are silent, and objects that had been moving stop. Another strange phenomenon is that when my husband would speak, the appearances would disappear immediately at the sound of his voice, without him saying any particular thing. It was like he had some power of authority over them. He didn't use any religious sayings or the name of God to rebuke the power that was over me. It wasn't long before I totally leaned on my husband to make the evil leave me. All he had to do was speak and the evil left. The only problem was, it always came back!

I could not, for the life of me, understand what was going on. This was the beginning of twenty-one long, miserable years of continuous harassment nearly every night, regardless of where we lived or the house. They found me and I didn't know or have the slightest idea of what to do to get out of this dilemma.

It didn't take very long and I had a very bad spirit of fear on me. I was already afraid of the dark and would sleep with a light on because I didn't want to be in total darkness. I had no peace at night. I couldn't even lay my head down on a pillow at night and rest without being tormented. One evening as I lay in bed, I felt fingers playing with my hair. Sometimes it would pull hard and at other times it would just stroke my hair. At other times, something would grab my arm and throw it up into the air, pinch my legs, or grab my toes and squeeze them until I screamed. Some nights after I would fall asleep, just before dawn, a cold feeling would go all over my body and an awful presence would be lying on top of me. I would scream, "My God, help me! I want out of this situation!" I felt in my heart that I didn't do anything evil to anyone to deserve this kind of punishment, but I couldn't find a way out.

As time passed, I started seeing faces on the walls of our room at night. Pictures turned into the face of a skull. The head of a pirate with his black hat on, a patch over his eye, and rosy cheeks sat on the top of my chest of drawers and glared at me. Any clothing that would be laid down on a chair or vanity for the night would take the form of a person's body. Each night, before I went to bed, I folded my clothing and put it on the floor, hoping I wouldn't see anything else. But, nothing helped.

When I would try to talk to my husband about these things, he would tell me that I was crazy and was having hallucinations. He couldn't believe what I was telling him because he hadn't experienced anything. He couldn't see, feel, or hear anything that was happening to me, even though he slept right beside me, night after night.

By now Satan had found my weakness. **Fear!** He moved in on my weakness with all intense maneuvers he could and without me having the blood covering of Jesus Christ over me. Not being a born-again Christian, Satan had every legal right to harass me. But, thank God, God's plan was that Satan could not kill me! With this happening to me over and over again, I started asking a lot of questions wherever I went of anyone who would listen to me. I talked to my relatives, friends, neighbors, and even my doctor. Some gave me this terrific word: **"Don't tell anyone that you are seeing demons or they will think you are crazy and lock you up!" No one and I mean no one wanted to listen to me or give me an answer of comfort, knowledge, wisdom, understanding, or encouragement. Everyone just wanted me to shut up.**

I was shunned, ridiculed, mocked, and made fun of. No one wanted to be around me. But even with that, I still didn't give up. I knew that I knew that somewhere, somehow, there was an answer that would free me of this horrible situation. I kept pressing in, even if it was the wrong direction. It was better to keep trying even if I failed. I heard a doctor say one time, "It is better to try and fail, than it is to fail to try." So I continued my search.

The Jehovah Witnesses told me that the devil was attacking me because I wasn't doing the will of God. I didn't know it then, but I truly wasn't. What they meant was I wasn't in the field service as I was supposed to be. I asked them to pray for me time and time again, but they wouldn't. They also told me they did not cast out devils, because all the miracles, healings, deliverances, and speaking in tongues were done away with when the last apostle died. I was instructed to go home, search through the house for anything that might look demonic. If I found anything that I believed a demon had taken up residence in, such things as antiques, old mirrors, and books, I was to burn them and everything would be all right.

To make everyone happy, I went home, searched my house for anything that fit that description, burned a few antique pictures, glasses, etc., but nothing happened. No change occurred! Was I defeated at this point? No, something inside of me said, DON'T GIVE UP and DON'T QUIT!

For years my husband went to the Kingdom Hall with me and the children. In the later years, he said he didn't believe their doctrine and would not continue to go with me very often. At my request, he agreed to take their test of eighty questions necessary to become a Jehovah Witness, but he flunked the test and they told me he was not ready to be a Jehovah Witness. Today, I can say, praise the Lord that he flunked that test. After that, I went alone with our two children to the meetings for years.

My husband and I were drifting so far apart from each other because neither one of us had the love of Jesus Christ in us. I still desired so much that we would be as a family and worship together, so I decided to study to become a Catholic. For a few months I studied that religion hoping it would help restore our marriage. But nothing changed in our relationship during this time. There was too much stress going on in our lives.

I talked to the priest about my problems. He responded kindly, but he said that he personally had never heard of such supernatural experiences. He felt that if I would go home and repeat ten Hail Mary's, count the rosary, put up palm branches, and hang a crucifix on the wall near our bed, more than likely, all the evil would leave. Again, I was willing to try anything, so I obeyed his advice to the letter. This was not the answer! That very night, the crucifix that was hanging on a nail in the wall fell on the tile floor with such a loud noise that it scared everyone in the house! And it kept getting worse! More and more evil spirits revealed themselves to me and to our children.

One night in particular, my little daughter started choking. Her face was turning blue and she couldn't get her breath. It was as if she had whooping cough. I didn't know what to do for her but cry. I was afraid she was going to die. We rushed her to the nearest hospital emergency room, and as soon as we got her into the doctor's room, it all left! They could find absolutely nothing wrong with her! If only I would have known then what I know now, I would have taken authority over that demonic spirit and it would not have attacked my daughter! Or if it had, I could have made it leave her by using the Word of God and the precious name of Jesus. But at that time, we were ignorant of the Word of God and of God's power against the enemy of our souls.

These evil spirit beings, sometimes in the form of men, women, or children, entered into our bedrooms and stood at the end of our beds. Either they walked up and down the hallways or just stood in the doorways and stared at us. Some wouldn't move for hours. I would see them and turn away, then look back later to see if they were still there and they were. They wouldn't leave. After a while, I just accepted them because hardly a night passed that I was not visited by their evil presence.

Believe me, these were not angels sent by God. I even got to the point that I accused my husband of making these things happen to us, because he was still free of the torment that the children and I were going through eight years later. But he would always answer me that he wouldn't do that to me or to anyone else. I don't know how anyone could hate another person so bad that they would do this terrible thing.

In 1965 we moved to California due to a transfer in employment. We bought a beautiful home in Hacienda Heights. I had a few months of peace and I thought, *Hooray, it's over!* I was so extremely happy I could hardly contain myself. But it was short-lived. They found me!

I remember late one night, my husband went to bed early and I stayed up to watch a late movie. After it was over, I went into the bedroom, undressed, and climbed into bed. Then, I laid my head on my husband's chest, facing the closet. The door was open slightly and suddenly out came this large seven-foot tall form of a man with a hood over his head. I could see that it was wearing a cape over his shoulders, but he had no face. In his hands, he had a scarf which he twisted around and around as if he were going to put it around my neck. He kept gliding back and forth across the floor at the end of the bed. I started screaming at my husband, saying, "Wake up, wake up! I'm not sleeping this time. I know it's real! He wants to kill me! Say something!"

Oscar just lay there as if in a deep sleep and didn't murmur a word. I beat on his chest so hard to make him speak. I'm surprised I didn't break his ribs. I continued pleading for him to speak while the spirit moved back and forth. Within minutes, I was frantically screaming and crying, saying, "Say something!" Finally, he said, "All right, all right, I hear you!" Immediately the spirit took two huge steps and went right through the wall and disappeared. This was the turning point in my husband's life. Not mine, but his.

By morning, my husband was thoroughly convinced that I was ready for the insane asylum. He determined that I was crazy, and he called my mom in Oklahoma and told her to come and get me. Enough was enough! He had all he could take of me. I didn't even try to stop him, because now I almost believed it myself. But in my heart, I knew I wasn't crazy! I just didn't know why this was happening to me. I knew that I was actually seeing these things. I didn't know how to get out of it! This was something I didn't ask for or want or desire to have. But it was there and I had to deal with it.

I pleaded with Oscar not to send me to a mental hospital. I told him, **"I wish just one time it would happen to you so you would believe me!"** I wanted him to know and feel what I had gone through all those years. I wanted him to know I had been telling him the truth. I'm here to warn you, look out what you confess over another person.

That very night as we lay in our bed just staring at the ceiling and not speaking to each other because of what was happening and what was said during the day from both of us, another attack of the enemy hit us hard. Suddenly, out of nowhere, a huge form of a spider filled the size of the 10x11 bedroom. It came down from the ceiling, waving its many legs at us. This time my husband saw it and he screamed so loud and was so scared he fell out of bed onto the floor. Of course, with the scream, the spider left. By morning, though, he had convinced himself that it was just a nightmare. It really didn't happen, and as a result of that decision, I was still leaving! My heart sank! I felt so sure that if it happened to him, just once, that he would believe me and he wouldn't send me away. I knew that all hope was lost until the following morning.

Before he left for work, he went into the bathroom to shower and shave. He shut the door behind him as he went in. As he started to shave, a strong gust of wind engulfed him from out of the corner of the room. He staggered out of the bathroom and came into the bedroom where I was still in bed. His eyes were as big as eggs and his Mexican hair stood on end! He said, "Okay, okay, I believe you! Now, what are we going to do about it?" He was now ready to take action!

We felt that a more drastic measure needed to be taken than any other time before. At this point of confusion, we jumped from the frying pan into the fire! We had tried the Jehovah Witnesses and a Catholic priest. Where else do we go?

There are some well-meaning people in this world. A woman I worked with told me of a fortune-teller she knew who lived in a nearby community. For only a small amount of money, say $3.00, she could help us get rid of the demons since she dealt with the spirit world. I was told she didn't deal with black magic. She only practiced white magic. So we went to see Mama so-and-so (the name has been changed to protect me). We hoped in our hearts that we weren't doing any wrong, because I knew it was against God's will to inquire of a fortune-teller, but at this point, we were desperate.

We then made arrangements through the co-worker to go visit with the fortune-teller. We arrived at her house late at night when no one could see us. When we entered into the living room, I told her immediately that we didn't want to do anything against God. She assured us of the good she was doing and that she also believed in God (although she didn't stress which god she was referring to).

Immediately, she started revealing things to us by going into a trance. She told me that a curse of witchcraft had been put on me years ago, and unless the curse was broken, she saw my husband with another woman and me with another man. She said that an Indian had burned $150.00 to place the curse on me, and she needed that amount of money to burn so the curse could be broken. We agreed to bring the finances she asked for, believing this was our way out.

A few days later we went to her home again. She invited us in again and took us into her kitchen area. She gave us a glass, placed an egg in a handkerchief, wrapped it up, and put it in the glass. She then told us to put the glass under our bed for three days. She told us that it would catch the thing that had been after me and would break the spell. Then she proceeded to turn our backs to her while she supposedly burned the money. With a quick move of the hand, it looked like the real money went into a pocket of her apron, and some play money was placed on the fork over the stove burner. But who cares what happened to the money? We wanted freedom at any cost! As it burned, she turned us around and said, "See, the curse will be broken!"

We then took the glass home and placed it under the bed. During the next three days, our dog went wild in the house. He growled and snarled at our bed and tried to get under it. We had to put the dog outside. He ran from one side of the house to the other, trying to get in. At the end of the third day, we took the glass back to Mama so-and-so. She took the wrapped handkerchief out of the glass and told my husband to crush the egg gently with his foot on the floor. As he did, she picked it up and started separating the white from the yolk. Inside of the egg was a little black object that resembled a small bear claw, about an inch long. She told me that she had caught the animal that was after me!

Then she asked us if we had done any evil to anyone. We replied, "No!" We had no known enemies, so she took a dollar bill and tore it in half in front of us, and then she crumbled the two halves together and gave it to my husband to keep in his pocket for three days. If we had done no evil to anyone, we were told that the divided dollar would return to its original form, not torn. So, still believing this was the answer to our problem, Oscar carried the crumpled dollar bill in his pants pocket for the next three days. When we went back to see her, Oscar gave her the bill. She slowly unfolded it before our eyes and to our surprise, the dollar bill was intact!

So what happened next? Of course, she needed more money for the exorcism! There needed to be an additional burning of another $150.00 and we would have to pay the extra if we wanted to keep the curse away. At that time, we didn't have any more extra money for this project, but we were going to find a way to get it.

That night as we entered our home, the hallway appeared as if there was a fog at the end of it. There seemed to be a smell of a very bad odor. No one wanted to go into their bedrooms, so we took the children (we had two at this time) and we spent the night with Oscar's mother, who lived in East Los Angeles. As best as I can remember, my husband's relatives helped us with the added money we needed because it scared them for us even to talk about such things that we were going through.

We took the additional money to Mama so-and-so and she told us that her part was completed now. She related to us that the one dollar bill that had been torn was going to be used to win us a sweepstakes worth $50,000.00. Did we believe this "crock of macaroni"? Yes, I'm sorry to say!

We had lived over eight years in this tormenting situation of haunted houses and we wanted out! And the $50,000.00 looked pretty good too! Funny though, another woman with five children who was friends with the woman who introduced us to the fortune-teller bought our beautiful home quickly for a little of nothing. Even though she knew what we had gone through in the house, she was not afraid to move in! This beautiful home cost us only $11,000.00. We sold it for $200.00, then moved and our payments were $113.00 a month. Now, twenty-six years later, it's probably worth over $200,000.00 or $300,000.00. Wow! Did we pay a heavy price for listening to other people with bad counsel!

My mom arrived at our home a few days later, but she returned to Oklahoma without me. At least that part was gained. Within a few weeks, we moved back to Oklahoma. We moved into a rental house belonging to my mom on her acreage in McLoud where I grew up. We didn't have a phone right away, so my mom took any phone calls for me and relayed the messages. Mama so-and-so called us, but my mom declined to tell us. She took matters into her own hands and threatened Mama so-and-so that if she didn't return all of our money we had given to her, my mom was going to call the police on her and have her arrested. I had told my mom what had transpired while we were living in California. So being a mom, she took our problems upon herself and took further action.

Needless to say, the bottom fell out of us getting rich quick. We were supposed to have met a man who had our winning ticket number and we would have paid for it with that special dollar. But now it was called off! As weeks passed, we began receiving $50.00 money orders until $350.00 was paid. But the evil didn't cease! In this house, it was far greater than any other place we had ever lived. Matters got worse. It was like all hell and double hockey sticks broke loose against us.

My mom, still a Jehovah Witness, encouraged the Witnesses to have a Bible study with me because of all of my problems. I agreed, since I was still seeking help from any angle. I told the woman who studied with me the problems we were dealing with, and to tell you the truth, I was sick and a nervous wreck. She told me not to be afraid and if I saw anything else, to look straight at it and command the things I saw and felt to "leave me in the name of Jehovah"! All I had to do from then on was to do the will of God, which was to go door-to-door witnessing, using the literature of the Watchtower and Tract Society. Then, it would totally stop! What insight this woman had! I wonder why I had not thought of that. Did it work? Partly, but partly was not good enough for me. I wanted a complete end to the demonic harassment, but it was not yet in sight.

I was about seven months pregnant with our third child and sometimes it wasn't unusual for me and our five-year-old son to lie down in the afternoon and take a nap. This time it was early in the morning after my husband left for work. For some odd reason, I was very, very sleepy. As I lay in bed, I immediately went to sleep and I began to dream. In my dream, I dove into a swimming pool and instead of coming back up to the surface, I was going deeper and deeper, running out of air.

Immediately as I was waking up from the dream, I realized there was numbness over all my body and I could not move my little finger or an eyelash. I could still feel, think, and hear, but I just couldn't move. Then all of a sudden I felt the tips of fingers crawling up my chest one at a time, all the way to my throat. Then a hand grabbed me around my throat and started choking me. It squeezed so hard I couldn't breath. All I could do was think in my mind, "LEAVE ME IN THE NAME OF JEHOVAH!"

Within a matter of seconds, the hand started pulling away from my throat. Instantly the numbness left. Then, I sat up on the edge of my bed and cried. I thanked Jehovah God for sparing my life at that time. Being in the spiritual condition I was in, had I died at that time, the Bible says in Romans 6:23, **"For the wages of sin is death; but the gift of God is eternal life through Jesus Christ our Lord."** Romans 10:13 says, **"For whosoever shall call upon the name of the Lord shall be saved."**

My little boy sat up on the bed crying and crying and said to me, "Mama, a while ago my throat hurt me so bad I couldn't hardly stand it! But it doesn't hurt now!" I put my arms around him and hugged him tightly and told him, "Son, you won't ever hurt like that anymore, I promise you because I know now who our real protector is. It is not your daddy. It is God! God will watch over us from now on!"

God was always there for me, I just didn't know it! This was a turning point in my life where I stopped trusting man and started trusting God! Even though I learned to call on the name of Jehovah many times, the harassment still continued. When I would see anything again, I pointed my finger at it and commanded, **"In the name of Jehovah God, leave me!"** The figures or presence would leave immediately for a while, but always came back. The fear wasn't as great as before, since I knew that Jehovah God was with me and would protect me.

Many times throughout the years, I talked to neighbors, friends, relatives, or anyone who would listen to me as I sought an answer to this terrifying problem. Many laughed at me, ridiculed me, and told me not to tell anyone about this problem because they would think that I was crazy. I believe now in this hour there is so much evidence of similar demonic supernatural experiences that people are or have been going through, that it is the time to write this book, because now there will be understanding of what I am talking about without the doubt of my sanity.

Forty years ago, this was not experienced by many people except maybe in third world countries. But now, times have changed! Some people said it was my imagination, that I really wasn't seeing those things. Others just didn't believe me and thought it was a joke. The problem was, I wasn't laughing! No one wants to hear or talk about these types of experiences.

Once people found out what was happening to me, I was the least welcome person around. It was embarrassing to my family to speak of this evil happening to us, but I was desperate. And when you get desperate enough in a situation, you will seek help, even if it's the wrong help! Still, no one had the right answer. Shall we try behind "door number three"?

As more years passed, the tension (people call it stress these days) grew in our family. I was a total wreck. While I was pregnant the third time, I was very concerned for our unborn child as to the effect my condition would have on him if any. I sat in the doctor's office and twisted a handkerchief around my fingers, so nervous I couldn't sit still. I was afraid to talk to him, but I still needed help. Tears rolled down my face as I spoke to the doctor about an evil spirit entering into my baby through me. I was at my wit's end.

This kind of questioning was not routine to this doctor, and he explained that he had no knowledge of what was happening to me or what to do about it. But he did suggest that he had a close friend who was a psychiatrist and perhaps he could help me. I told him that I did not have the money to pay him per hour, so he proposed that he would make a tape of our conversation and he would send it to him. Hopefully, by the next visit, the psychiatrist would have enlightened me on the subject. Needless to say, this was agreeable to me. So I related the whole story to my doctor, which he recorded.

The following week at my next visit, my regular doctor had done just as he had promised, and he spoke to his friend. In response to the tape, the psychiatrist exclaimed that after listening to the tape, since I was of Spanish descent with ancestors from Mexico, probably all of this witchcraft came from there, and since I believed it, <u>I would just have to live with it</u>! These men, although well-educated, brilliant, intelligent men, had neither a clue nor a logical explanation of what was happening to me. Then I felt that all hope was gone forever of being set free from this demonic oppression. To my knowledge there was no way out! A few weeks later, I delivered a healthy, beautiful, normal little boy. I truly thanked God for this.

As time passed, I continued with sickness. I went to the doctor and found out through many tests that I had ulcers and hypoglycemia (low blood sugar). With this stigma added to our relationship, it seemed like all was not well! It was truly hard raising my family under such conditions.

Several months later, we decided to move back to California where there were better jobs and my husband's family. We took our three children and our furnishings and left Oklahoma. Even though it seemed as if we were living in an impossible condition, so to speak, we stayed together, not giving up hope of finding the way out of this nightmare that was now affecting all of the family. In my heart, I knew we had to have love for each other to have gone through this and not be separated. I can see now that God was with us, even in our ignorance. God's grace and His mercy were upon us even then.

As we drove the rental truck and our car through the streets of Montebello, California, we pulled into a grocery store parking lot to go inside to look at a bulletin board for any houses for rent. Would you believe there was a house for rent one block from the store we were at? We called the owner of the house, met her there and within the hour, rented her house! I don't believe things like this are coincidental. I had to believe that God was still on our side.

While we lived in Montebello, Oscar held down several jobs to support our growing family. I had another beautiful daughter while living there and was getting more involved with the Jehovah's Witnesses again, going stronger than ever before. My children and I attended many of the meetings, but most of the time without their dad. When I had a Bible study at home, Oscar slipped out the back door and stayed gone until the people left. Then he would return home.

I wanted my children to grow up loving Jehovah God like I did, even if I had to force it upon them. They were very disciplined children during all the meetings and even at the conventions where we would stay all day. There was no nursery to take your children to and drop them off like other churches have today. We were responsible for the actions of our children. Of course, I was a very strict, religious woman. If they needed correction, I took them to the restroom like everyone else did and spanked them. Our five children soon learned how to sit still during the services. Would you believe, I even carried a switch from a tree in my handbag?

One evening at a meeting we were attending, my cute little mischief maker found the switch and said, "Ha, ha, Mama, look what I found?" Then he proceeded to break it into pieces. I replied, "Ha, ha, look what Mama is going to do. Let's go get another one!" I quietly dragged him down the aisle to go outside with him screaming at the top of his lungs, "Mama, I love you! Mama, I love you!" Did that stop Mama? No! I got outside, found me another tree, broke off a little switch, and gave him three licks with it. I had no problem with not sparing the rod as the Bible tells us to do. I thank God though, I did not spank him in anger.

Chapter 7

FALLING AWAY

After living in California for a year, we took a vacation back to Oklahoma to see our friends and relatives. While we were there, my aunt told us of a small acreage she thought was for sale. Wow! Did we get excited about having our own little plot of ground. My husband always wanted to live on a farm because he was raised in El Paso, Texas, in town. He always talked about the story book of Dick and Jane on the farm. So here was our chance!

My aunt took us to the acreage and we went up to the front door of the house and knocked. A woman appeared at the door, and my aunt boldly asked her if her property was for sale! The woman stammered and then said, "Well, yes, we have been talking about it." We proceeded to ask her lots of questions about the sale and with my aunt's help, we bought that acreage! Ten acres and a little house, barn, cellar, etc. for only $16,000.00, and my husband didn't even have a job when we moved back to Oklahoma! Can you see a move of God in this transaction?

My aunt also helped us buy our first milk cow and two baby pigs to get us started. But the big problem we were having was, the jobs for my husband were not that plentiful and we lived about twenty-five miles from the city. So I had to go to work outside the home to help with the income. Oscar got some part-time jobs, but surprisingly enough, one day an unexpected insurance check came in the mail. With it, Oscar decided to go to Truck Driving School. He was bound and determined he wanted to drive a truck cross-country and that he did. It was truly hard for me to raise the children by myself, because he was gone most of the time, sometimes as long as two to three weeks at a time, and only home two or three days before he went out again.

At one time when he was at home, our little boy, four years old at the time, looked up at his daddy and said, "Daddy, do you really live he-ah?" Out of the mouth of babes! His trucking career lasted for twenty-eight long years. We had many of my relatives living around us who helped when I needed it, but living alone with the five children was certainly a hard task!

After about seventeen years of driving, trucking didn't have that glow anymore, and Oscar wanted to do something to get off the road. He wanted to be home with the remaining family who hadn't grown up and moved away. So he decided to purchase a little grocery store/filling station about twenty-five miles away out in the country. He thought as soon as it was profitable, he would quit the trucking job and stay home and run the store. We agreed on this maneuver and we mortgaged our acreage to pay for groceries, gasoline, and rental of the building.

We also purchased a mobile home and moved it next to the store. This worked out more satisfactorily as we were close to the store and I didn't have to drive to get there. We sold all of our animals and rented our home. To all appearances, this sounded like we were getting on the winning side of this thing, but what we didn't know almost killed me. I sincerely believe that this was the place in our lives that the devil thought that he was going to put us totally into Hades forever, but praise the Lord, this was the beginning of deliverance for us.

Four years passed and I continued to manage the store. Our sons helped me with all of the work in the evening after school and weekends when my husband wasn't home. I had my small son with me at all times, and sometimes it was difficult to change a diaper and check out a customer at the cash register! But most of the people knew our needs and were quite friendly. In fact, I made lot of friends, good and bad!

We hired a few employees for the times I had to go to the city to buy groceries at the warehouse or the produce plant, but it really wasn't enough. There was so much tension when Oscar came home from his trips. We struggled in this store financially and soon Oscar had to stay on the road just to keep groceries in the store. We allowed several customers to have credit and when they couldn't or wouldn't pay their bill, we got behind in our obligations. We got so far behind in our house payments that the banker was going to foreclose on us. We didn't know what to do. Oscar accused me of bad management and the condition of our relationship grew worse.

Since we now know Christ is the Silent Listener to every conversation, we also know that Satan hears every word you say, too. At this point, I believe Satan sent out his troops to kill, steal, or destroy us in a few more ways that hadn't been tried yet! Since the love of Jesus did not prevail in our home and we were just showing hate all the time in word and action, not caring for one another, we left the door open for total destruction of our marriage. We spoke of divorce several times, but we didn't have the money for it! And where would I go with five children?

During this particular time, an older man started coming into our store to purchase gasoline. Every day he came and each day he began to compliment me. He had very flattering words that really lifted me up. I needed to hear those kind of words, but not from someone other than my husband. It wasn't long and I believed everything this man told me. I fell like a ton of bricks for this man and never would I have dreamed that I would fall, because I was so strong in my faith in Jehovah God. I was wrong! Satan knew my weakness and he really worked on it! I needed love so much, I got to the point I didn't even care about anyone else, I just wanted to know that I was loved and appreciated. So I went to the bottom of the pit. Then I hated myself.

Something inside of me kept saying, "Emma, this is not the way!" There is no happiness in sin! Yes, it may be fun for a season, but after a while I wanted to commit suicide. I kept hearing voices telling me to kill myself because no one cared for me, and I believed it! I had so much hate, bitterness, anger, and rejection, and probably many other evils inside of me, I couldn't even think straight.

One day after I had returned from one of the conventions of the Jehovah Witnesses, I decided I wanted out of this situation that I had gotten myself into. I had to tell someone I needed help. I went to a brother in the Jehovah Witness belief whom we knew and fellowshipped with and told him my story. He said that I needed to talk to an elder. The elder at the Kingdom Hall then arranged a meeting of three other elders and three witnesses to listen to my case. They asked me all kinds of questions about my life and made me go into detail as to what had happened. I truly was sorry for my actions. I broke down and wept bitterly before the men, and I asked Jehovah God to forgive me of all of my sins.

One of the elders said that he had never seen anyone who was as repentant as I was. After hours of talking to them, they took into consideration the way my husband had treated me mentally, emotionally, and physically. This abuse was hard for me to take, plus living with this terror in my life from a curse! As a result, they did not disfellowship me from the congregation, but they put me on a six-month probation. With this ruling, no one in the congregation could speak, eat, or fellowship with me for a six-month period of time. I could only talk to the elders. They also told me that I could not go witnessing anymore or take part in any of the services.

Can you imagine what I felt like? More rejection! Now, I really felt alone, unloved, unwanted, discouraged, and the thought of death looked pretty good to me. This sentence of correction on me was announced to the whole congregation. People who had come to our home for cookouts and picnics and our children went to school together, could no longer even look me in the face. To them I had committed the unpardonable sin! If they saw me on the sidewalk, they went to the other side of the street so as not to have to pass by me! I felt like an outcast, a leper, if you will. It had to have been the grace of God that kept me alive because there was no hope anywhere. The Witnesses just made it worse for me. The entire congregation rejected me.

I felt worse than dirt under their feet. I didn't understand why they had the right to judge me that way.

Galatians 6:1-2 says:

Brethren, if a man be overtaken in a fault, ye which are spiritual, restore such an one in the spirit of meekness; considering thyself, lest thou also be tempted.

Bear ye one another's burdens, and so fulfill the law of Christ.

James 5:19-20 NKJV says:

Brethren, if anyone among you wanders from the truth, and someone turns him back, let him know that he who turns a sinner from the error of his way will save a soul from death and cover a multitude of sins.

According to these scriptures, I was not treated as brethren with any form of mercy or love. I just received condemnation and judgment. Even Jesus did not come to condemn the world, but to save it.

Once a year at the Kingdom Hall, they held what they called a Memorial Service. In this they celebrate the Lord's Supper, which included the sharing of the unleavened bread and wine, representing the body and blood of our dear Lord Jesus Christ. Of course, if you were not one of the 144,000 chosen ones, you were not to partake of the emblems. I never could figure it out that in all the years that I was a Jehovah Witness, I never saw but one woman eat of the bread and drink of the wine. I asked her how she knew that she was one of the chosen ones, and she told me that Jehovah God had told her. She was knowledgeable in their doctrine. But I was in confusion because Revelation 7:4 says, **"And I heard the number of them which were sealed: and there were sealed an hundred and forty and four thousand of all the tribes of the children of Israel."** The 144,000 are described as bondservants of God from the tribes of the sons of Israel. God will set a seal or a mark upon their foreheads to indicate consecration and ownership. Some Bible interpreters believe these new believers from among the sons of Israel will be commissioned and empowered by the Holy Spirit to preach the gospel during the Tribulation days. I believe what the Bible says, not man.

I knew I was not a Jew, nor had works for me to partake of the emblems of the Lord's Supper, but something happened to me when the plate of unleavened bread was placed into my hands. A voice spoke to me and said, ***"Take and eat, for this is My body."*** I started crying and shaking all over. I wanted to take of our Lord's Supper, but I knew I was unworthy. I definitely knew I was not one of the chosen ones (the 144,000) in the Kingdom Hall. Anyway, through my tears, I pushed the plate to the next person who didn't partake either. Then, a few minutes later, the cup of wine, representing the blood of Jesus, was passed to each person. The same voice came to me again as I accepted the cup into my hands, saying, ***"Take, drink, for this is My blood!"*** I shoved it to the person beside me so fast that it almost spilled on the floor. I could hardly keep the tears back. I didn't understand any of the meaning of communion. I had never taken communion before in all of my life, but something inside of me wanted to very much.

Now, over thirty to thirty-five years later, after I was saved, while attending Ted Holloway's Fellowship in Maysville, Oklahoma, after he preached the Word of God, he wanted the congregation to take communion. What a joy rose up in me! I knew I needed to do this even if I didn't have all the understanding of what it meant. I knew it was the right thing to do. Pastor Ted opened the Bible to 1 Corinthians 11:23-32 and read:

**For I have received of the Lord that which also
I delivered unto you, that the Lord Jesus the same
night in which he was betrayed took bread:**

And when he had given thanks, he brake it, and said, Take, eat: this is my body, which is broken for you: this do in remembrance of me.

After the same manner also he took the cup, when he had supped, saying, This cup is the new testament in my blood: this do ye, as oft as ye drink it, in remembrance of me.

For as often as ye eat this bread, and drink this cup, ye do shew the Lord's death till he come.

Wherefore whosoever shall eat this bread, and drink this cup of the Lord, unworthily, shall be guilty of the body and blood of the Lord.

But let a man examine himself, and so let him eat of that bread, and drink of that cup.

For he that eateth and drinketh unworthily, eateth and drinketh damnation to himself, not discerning the Lord's body.

For this cause many are weak and sickly among you, and many sleep.

For if we would judge ourselves, we should not be judged.

But when we are judged, we are chastened of the Lord, that we should not be condemned with the world.

The plate of unleavened bread and a small cup of grape juice (some churches use this instead of wine) were passed to the congregation, one waiting upon another until all had received. Then our prayers of repentance were expressed before we took the blessed sacraments. We examined ourselves for known or secret sins we needed to put under the blood of Jesus before we commenced. Then it was time. Oh, glory! Did I cry! I put that piece of bread in my mouth, representing the broken body of Christ Jesus, and I just could not contain myself. Then we were told to drink the juice that represented Jesus' precious blood. Oh, my! Tears of joy flooded my soul. I don't remember how long I cried. It was like a new birth. I felt so refreshed and healed. It was one of the most wonderful experiences I had ever had spiritually. I recommend it to you! Jesus says "Do it in remembrance of Me!"

Now, back to my sentence of correction from the elders of the Kingdom Hall of Jehovah Witnesses. Six months passed, then seven, and I went to the elders to see if my sentence had been lifted from me. To my surprise, the particular elder who had placed the six-month penalty on me had died before he released me. When the time came for my release, it was not the same anymore. The people did not change their attitudes toward me. You could see by the countenance of their faces that they had not forgiven me. But, glory to God! God forgave me when I asked Him to forgive me.

Chapter 8

MY MIRACULOUS HEALING

One afternoon, both my husband and I were working in the store and one of our regular customers and a friend, Sue Bailey, came in. She asked us if we would like to go to her church and hear a message on faith healing. At this time, I was so sick of being sick, I was willing to try almost anything. Of course, I told her that I didn't believe in faith healing and I didn't understand this type of faith. But my husband wanted to go to hear the message. I had to take into consideration my religion because we were not supposed to fellowship with other people in their church or denomination. But since it was out in the country, I didn't think I would get caught, so we went!

As we entered this beautiful ranch home of Pastor Ted Holloway, I sensed a different atmosphere than in the Kingdom Hall of Jehovah Witnesses. I felt warmth, love, and peace that I had never felt before. Something was totally different about the entire place. We were warmly greeted by the pastor's precious wife, Karen, and everyone in the small congregation, then we sat down.

The pastor took his place and offered prayer to God. Then we entered into a time of beautiful praise and worship unlike I had ever experienced before. I didn't know how to feel the presence of God in a place, but something was in that room that was so awesome, so peaceable, so refreshing. I had never been in that type of atmosphere before. It's hard to describe when you have gone through so much turmoil, and then just enter a place and a peace just falls on you. You ask, "What is happening to me?" You really don't want to leave! I didn't know what to expect from this type of church. But, you know, it's not the church! It's the Spirit of God! I hadn't felt a move of God like that in all my life. It was beautiful, almost heavenly!

Then Pastor Ted introduced the evangelist, Joe Popell. He started talking about Jesus. He told us how Jesus went about healing all manner of sickness and disease. I listened attentively, but with my teaching for almost thirty-three years at that time, I had learned that all supernatural healings were done away with when the last of the apostles died and it was not for us today. But, you know, *I wished it would happen to me! I needed a miracle in my life!* I even said to myself in my thoughts, *I wish it would happen to me!*

God knows every thought that we have, and God wants to bless us more than we even want to be blessed! Just to show me that *He is God Almighty and He is love perfected,* He performed this miracle for me! He heard the cry of my heart and answered me even while I was an unbeliever and a sinner!

After a time of preaching the Word of God, the evangelist asked in closing his sermon if there was anyone in the room who was sick to come up to the front. He wanted to pray for the sick. For a minute or two, there was complete silence. No one moved one way or the other. Even though it had been several hours since I had last eaten and I was very nauseous and dizzy, I refused to go up front. I didn't believe in this "laying on of hands" and it scared me. I just stood there quietly, but held my hand over my mouth because I was so sick to my stomach. I didn't want to excuse myself and go to the restroom because I didn't want to interrupt the time of prayer.

Then he said again, "Okay, if anyone here is sick or hurting, put your hand where you hurt, and we are going to pray!" At that point, I thought to myself, *The doctors haven't helped me, the medicine hasn't helped me, and now what do I have to lose?* Then I put my hand across my stomach. He began to pray.

A passage of his prayer went like this: **"And Satan, I bind you and rebuke you, you spirit of infirmity. Leave in the name of Jesus!"** Before the prayer was even finished, I felt a sensation of a band about six inches wide, draw from my left side, pull across my stomach and lift off. All nausea and dizziness that I had earlier left me immediately! Within seconds, all of my sickness was gone! Glory to God! I started moving my head back and forth. I couldn't believe what had happened to me.

My little daughter, who was standing next to me, said, "Mama, what's the matter?" I said to her, "Mary, I'm not sick anymore! I'm not sick anymore!" I wanted to cry! Then the evangelist asked if anyone felt any better.

Naturally, I wanted to say that something supernatural happened to me, so I raised my hand. He then asked me to come up front and tell the congregation what had happened. I walked up to the altar and he said, "What happened to you, little lady?" I told them that I had been sick for over twenty-one years and during the prayer, the sickness left. No person laid a hand on me. It was all supernatural! I couldn't understand what happened, but I knew that I wasn't sick anymore. All of the congregation clapped and praised God! I heard one little grandma in the front say, "It's a miracle!" Yes, truly it was a divine, instant miracle! God touched my physical body to open my eyes to tell me that His Word is real and alive even today, just as it was two thousand years ago.

But God still wasn't through with me yet. He was still working in my behalf! I didn't know how to have faith for a healing or a miracle in my body, so I knew it was totally God who did this miracle in me even though I was still an unbeliever! The evangelist asked me if I hurt anywhere else in my body. I then told him that I had been having a lot of back problems and had been going to a chiropractor for many years. He told me to sit down in a chair, and he proceeded to lift both of my feet upward and said that I had one leg longer than the other. "We're going to pray," he said. So we bowed our heads and he began to pray. Within seconds, I felt a stretching motion in my left leg and it moved to the length of the right one. Again, I couldn't believe what was happening to me. I even accused the evangelist of moving my leg! Everyone laughed because they knew it was another miracle of God.

For several days, my left leg ached so bad that I thought something bad had happened, but then suddenly all of the pain left me, including the backaches! I went to the chiropractor once after my healing (incidentally, he was a Jehovah Witness), and while I was being treated, I shared my testimony with him of how God healed me! Whether he believed me or not, I don't know, but I sure gave God the glory!

As days and months passed, I wasn't sick anymore. I began to believe what had happened to me was truth. God had healed me divinely. Soon, I started asking Jehovah's Witnesses about healing. This was something we never talked about. A woman told me that she had heard of someone who claimed they had gotten healed, but they lost it. Strangely enough, I kept my healing! As time passed, I ate anything I wanted, when I wanted, and even fasted for days without getting sick. No more medication, shots, or bland diets for me. Even to this day, twenty-three years later, I am without sickness in my body and I take no medication! Glory to God!

I started telling everyone I met, regardless of where I was, how God had healed me, whether they believed it or not. It was truth, and I had great joy sharing it. These miracles and healings sure made a believer out of me! I wanted more of God's touch in my life, and I was hungry for the truth of God's Word! It was so wonderful not to wake up sick anymore. I had energy and strength I hadn't had for years! It had been so many long, miserable years.

One afternoon, our Christian friend, Sue, came into the store and asked me if I wanted to go with her again to a Women's Aglow meeting at her church to learn about the Holy Spirit. Of course, now that I knew the hand of God healed me, I wanted to know more. So I called another employee to come to work for me.

On the way to the church, which was about sixteen miles away, I shared with Sue what was heavy on my heart. I told her I really needed to know that someone loved me just like I was. I knew I had lived an unrighteous life for a while, and I had so much hate for myself and everyone else, and I didn't know how to get out of this situation! Man, did I have problems! I had not felt the kind of love I needed to sustain me to survive this life I was going through. I had to know that I was loved, or I still didn't want to live, regardless of the many miracles that I had received. I couldn't figure out that you don't get everything at one time, or just maybe you wouldn't be able to handle it all. So God had to work with me and work with me and work with me and work with me until He could get my attention! But Sue, being the compassionate person she is, just listened as I tearfully poured my heart out to her.

When we arrived at the church, all the women greeted each other and sat down. Suddenly the teacher, Phyllis Baker, spoke up and said, "The Lord has revealed to me that there is someone here who is under a lot of stress and oppression of the devil and the Holy Spirit is going to reveal who she is, and God is going to minister to her today!" I knew beyond a shadow of a doubt she was talking about me! My hopes rose to the highest expectation! I listened intently for over thirty minutes of teaching about the Holy Spirit, but I could hardly hold the tears back. I didn't know God was present in that place, already doing a work in me, but Matthew 18:20 says, **"For where two or three are gathered together in my name, there am I in the midst of them."**

After the teaching, all the women rose up and joined hands. We stood in a circle and they started praying in an unknown tongue and in English. The teacher broke the bond and walked directly over to me. She stood in front of me and grasped my hands. It was as if it was the Lord Jesus Christ Himself standing right there in front of me, looking me straight in the eyes, speaking with a strong voice of authority, boldness, and power, saying, **"God loves you! God loves you! He has chosen you to bring those out of the bondage that you have been in."**

She continued to prophesy (words of revelation given to her by the Holy Spirit) to me, but the words, <u>**God loves you**</u>, stuck in my heart like instant glue! **I knew that I knew beyond a shadow of a doubt that God loved me!** I knew she was telling the truth because I had just told Sue an hour before that I needed to know I was loved and no one else was in the car with us! So how did the teacher, Phyllis, know except the Holy Spirit revealed it to her? I didn't know any of the other women before that meeting except Sue. I could not stop crying.

Here are some of my *tears of joy* that I want to convey to you. Just knowing that God, our Creator of heaven and earth, loved me unconditionally gave me the desire to live and start all over! He knew I was bad, but I was one of the reasons for which He came to earth to live and die. Romans 5:8 reads, **"But God commendeth his love toward us, in that, while we were yet sinners, Christ died for us."** I gave up caring what other people thought or said about me, because now it was sown in my heart, **God loves me!** It didn't matter whether I was rejected, ridiculed, mocked, made fun of, or cursed. I had been given another chance to live and I intended to change! I didn't want to die anymore! I told Sue on the way home, **"I'm going to live, and proclaim the gospel of the Lord Jesus Christ just like He planned!"** I didn't even know what I was saying at that time, but it came out of my heart, and I meant every word. So be it!

I knew then that God had a specific plan for my life. I also knew had it not been for God watching over me all those years, I would not have had the strength to live through the trials I endured. I didn't know how to lean on Jesus. But through it all, God was with me and He continued to reveal Himself to me in many areas. From my weakest hour, even as a sinner, Jesus had His arms extended to me.

A Christian woman whom I went on a missionary trip with wept as I shared my testimony with the congregation. She asked the Lord, "Why am I crying over what she went through? I know by her testimony that she has overcome the trials." The Lord answered her by saying, **"I, too, wept over her!"** When she told me that, it so touched my heart to believe that Jesus wept over me. I know that He wept over His friend, Lazarus, when he died. But, who was I, that Jesus would weep over me? I was just another one of God's creation, and He loves me!

Chapter 9

BEATING, STROKE, HEART ATTACK, AND OUT-OF-BODY EXPERIENCE

With the decision in my heart to change, I knew what I had to do and I was going to do it, regardless of the consequences. Whatever we do in this life, good or bad, there are consequences that will come. How you receive and act upon them determine how you build your character. I had made up my mind and my heart for a new direction in my life, come hell or high water!

That afternoon, after coming home from the Bible study, I went to the store and started working for the remainder of the evening. The man I had been associated with came to get gas for his truck. I met him at the gas pump and told him to get back in his truck and never come back. He replied, "Oh, what's the matter? Did you find God?" I replied, "Yes, I found out that God loves me just like I am, and I'm ready for a change in my life. My old lifestyle is over!"

Needless to say, he left in a huff, but problems arose in his family as well as mine. This showed me that sin is no respecter of persons. It affects everyone.

About a week later, my husband came home from a trip and stayed home for a few days. He said to me that he had not seen the particular man around the store anymore and asked if I knew why. I said, "Yes, because I told him never to come back to our store anymore." My husband, being very inquisitive, asked, "Why not?" Being honest with my husband is what I thought I needed to do because I was tired of being deceitful. I told him I thought that I loved him. My husband replied, "You love him?"

Before I could answer him, uncontrolled anger that I had never seen in him rose up in him. He was so angry with me that he could not contain himself. I don't think that he realized the power he had within himself. Without even thinking about it, he threw back his fist and hit me so hard across the face that it sent me flying ten feet across the room and I hit the wall! Then, he proceeded to pick me up by the neck of my clothing and struck me again. I flew over our dining room table, landing in a chair. This was like something you would see in movies, except it was real, and it was happening to me!

I started going unconscious and I couldn't move. I heard him say, "If you get up, I'll do it again." He didn't know it, but I couldn't get up! I was hurt too bad. He was so hurt by my deceitful lifestyle that he called his brother in California and told him what had happened. He was told to take the children away from me and move there. His family would stand by him. He didn't know what to do after the call, so after he hung up the phone, he came over to me, grabbed hold of my weak body and dragged me into our bedroom and threw me on the bed. I didn't try to defend myself, even if I could have, because I felt that I needed to be punished for my actions.

I thank God every day that I don't have to take punishment like that anymore because Jesus paid the full price for my sins by dying on the cross and shedding His precious blood for you and me.

Unable to move, pain in my chest rose up within me. My husband, still in a rage of anger, was screaming at me to confess to him the life I had lived. He kept screaming at me "confess." I kept crying because I was in so much pain. No one even attempted to take me to the hospital and we didn't have 911 in the country. I didn't know how to pray, but in those last moments, I knew death was upon me. I cried out, **"Jehovah God, help me!"** That was all I could say, but I said it with all my heart! My chest was hurting so bad and the right side of my face started drawing toward my ear, and my tongue started swelling out of my mouth so that my tongue rested on the outside of my chin. My entire right side started paralyzing, my right hand drew up like a claw, and my leg began to go numb and draw up.

I was in so much pain, I couldn't cry anymore, and all of a sudden, when I closed my eyes, I wasn't in my body anymore. I wasn't in any more pain. I noticed I was wearing a little white robe, and I was inside of a very dark tunnel. I was flying at a terrific rate of speed upward. I could feel the breeze blowing my long black hair. I was looking upward as I spun through the tunnel. I didn't see any angelic beings around me. There was no glory, no peace, and I didn't see Jesus! But what I did see were the heavens and the stars at the top of the tunnel. All of a sudden, I was out of the tunnel and into the universe! There were billions (probably far more, I didn't count) of stars and planets. Then as I turned my head to look around, I thought to myself, *Well, there is the Milky Way,* just to name one of God's creations! I was just dangling in outer space like an astronaut!

As I turned to look further in the heavens, there was a mountain a short distance from me. Out of the top of this mountain came the most hideous hand and arm. It was gray in color, outlined in gold and silver around the hand, fingers, and arm. It was so evil looking, with long, pointed fingernails. The hand kept reaching out to get me, but it couldn't. I screamed, "The hand is trying to get me!"

I could hear my husband yelling at me, "You had better shut up. You're as close to death as you'll ever be." But when I opened my eyes, I was back in my bed, with severe pain in my body, and my husband was still yelling at me. I couldn't stop crying, but I could no longer speak! I know that I had the appearance of a person who had had a severe stroke. My little ten-year-old daughter, Mary, was sitting on the bed near me, stroking my hair and praying to God, "Please don't let Mama die!" I am here to tell you, **God answered her prayers. God hears the prayers of little children!**

My sons came from the other end of the mobile home, and said, "Daddy, please don't hurt Mama anymore! Mama, will you come and go with us to our bedroom?" I could not speak to give them an answer, but both boys came over to the bed and lifted me up, carried me to their room, and put me in their bed. Looking back now, I thank God that they didn't take me to the hospital because, had they done that, I would have missed out on the miracle God had planned for me!

John 10:10 states, **"The thief cometh not, but for to steal, and to kill, and to destroy: I am come that they might have life, and that they might have it more abundantly."** I believe that Satan had an assignment to kill me and to destroy my family, but **God had a greater plan for my life!** Jeremiah 29:11-14 reads:

> **For I know the thoughts that I think toward you, saith the LORD, thoughts of peace, and not of evil, to give you an expected end.**
>
> **Then shall ye call upon me, and ye shall go and pray unto me, and I will hearken unto you.**
>
> **And ye shall seek me, and find me, when ye shall search for me with all your heart.**
>
> **And I will be found of you, saith the LORD: and I will turn away your captivity, and I will gather you from all the nations, and from all the places whither I have driven you, saith the LORD; and I will bring you again into the place whence I caused you to be carried away captive.**

My son, Michael, said, "Mama, what can I do?" Without my answer to him, he said to me, "Mama, I'm going to read the Bible!" So he ran into the other room, found a Bible, and came back and knelt down beside the bed. He didn't even know where to look for any healing scriptures because we had never studied the Bible. We had been taught different, so we believed different! But that did not negate the Word of God, whether we believed it or not. God's Word is Truth! God had a much better plan for me than this, and it was about go into effect! Even though my son didn't know where to read in the Bible, the Holy

Spirit knew how to guide his little hands to the right place. He opened the Bible to Psalm 34:1-22 and read:

I will bless the LORD at all times: his praise shall continually be in my mouth.

My soul shall make her boast in the LORD: the humble shall hear thereof, and be glad.

O magnify the LORD with me, and let us exalt his name together.

I sought the LORD, and he heard me and delivered me from all my fears.

They looked unto him, and were lightened: and their faces were not ashamed.

This poor man cried, and the LORD heard him, and saved him out of all his troubles.

The angel of the LORD encampeth round about them that fear him, and delivereth them.

O taste and see that the LORD is good: blessed is the man that trusteth in him.

O, fear the LORD, ye his saints: for there is no want to them that fear him.

The young lions do lack, and suffer hunger: but they that seek the LORD shall not want any good thing.

Come, ye children, hearken unto me: I will teach you the fear of the LORD.

What man is he that desireth life, and loveth many days, that he may see good?

Keep thy tongue from evil, and thy lips from speaking guile.

Depart from evil, and do good: seek peace, and pursue it.

The eyes of the LORD are upon the righteous, and his ears are open unto their cry.

The face of the LORD is against them that do evil, to cut off the remembrance of them from the earth.

The righteous cry, and the LORD heareth, and delivereth them out of all their troubles.

The LORD is nigh unto them that are of a broken heart; and saveth such as be of a contrite spirit.

Many are the afflictions of the righteous; but the LORD delivereth him out of them all.

He keepeth all his bones; not one of them is broken.

Evil shall slay the wicked: and they that hate the righteous shall be desolate.

The LORD redeemeth the soul of his servants; and none of them that trust in him shall be desolate.

My son then shut the Bible and everything got quiet. All of a sudden, from the top of my head I felt a power move down my face. I cannot explain this to you other than the fact that my paralyzed face became pliable and returned to its natural, normal state. The swelling of my tongue totally decreased and my tongue returned back into my mouth. As this power continued down my body, the severe pain in my chest lifted off, continuing on down; my hand and fingers relaxed and straightened out, and continuing down, my leg stretched forth and all numbness left. **There was no more pain in my entire body!!!** I still didn't believe too much in miracles even though one had already happened to me, but to believe another would happen?

That was really stretching me! But now, beyond a shadow of a doubt, "I BELIEVE IN MIRACLES!" **Again, God used my little boy with his childlike faith to bring forth another miracle in my life for His glory! I give God the glory, thanksgiving, and praise for healing me!**

Psalm 107:19-22 NKJV says:

> **Then they cried out to the LORD in their trouble, and He saved them out of their distresses.**

> **He sent His word and healed them, and delivered them from their destructions.**

> **Oh, that men would give thanks to the LORD for His goodness, and for His wonderful works to the children of men!**

> **Let them sacrifice the sacrifices of thanksgiving, and declare His works with rejoicing.**

I know that I know that God heard my cry and sent His Word and healed me instantly! I just lay there quietly, and then I heard my husband coming down the hallway. He opened the door and said, "Honey, are you all right? Honey, I'm sorry. I'll never do that to you again. Will you come back and go to bed with me?" I said "yes" and I did. My little boy screamed at me, "No Mama, no!" But I told him, "Baby, it will be all right," and it was.

I believe that when God miraculously touched me with His healing virtue, God also touched my husband. God healed me for a purpose. He had a divine plan for my life that I did not know or was aware of. But I believe this was the greatest battle that I faced before my conversion to Christianity. Though I could not see it, more miracles and the goodness and the grace of God were ahead of me.

Chapter 10

OSCAR'S BATTLE WITH THE UNKNOWN AND HIS SALVATION

During the time we had the store, we bought a brick home two miles from there. It was located in the country too, down on a dead-end road, next to two Pentecostal families. Preachers lived in both of the houses! Does this look like a setup to you? I now call it, **"God's divine plan!"**

It was a battle to buy this house! It took five months, but it was so important that we buy this particular house because God was going to use this place for His divine intervention for our family! We didn't give up even though we didn't have a clue that this was God's plan! In His time, God would save, heal, and deliver us from the oppression that we had been under for over twenty-one years.

Of course, the devil didn't want us to move there, but we didn't want to live in the mobile home anymore. We had really gotten ourselves in a financial bind with the store, our acreage, and now this home. With our obligations, we were buried in debt. We had to put our acreage up for sale, but contracts with prospective buyers kept falling through. We didn't know where to turn.

I found out that during these hard times that God uses many people to bring others into His Kingdom. Deliverance can come in many ways if you are seeking God and if you truly want out of your situation. God uses different times, situations, people, and circumstances to aid you and to direct your path to Jesus. Even when I didn't know it, I was going toward Him, though I was stumbling all the way. When I fell, He was there to pick me up and strengthen me to not give up.

For many years after I wished my husband would see or experience the torment I had felt and seen, the harassment continued with all of the family. When my husband would come under attack by the evil spirits, he tried to wrestle with them instead of rebuking them in the name of Jesus. Sometimes it would take him as long as thirty minutes to overcome the power over him. He was defenseless. He told me that the attacks sometimes felt like jolts of electricity on his body. He felt powerless under the attacks. Now, I lay beside him this time, sound asleep, and I was not disturbed in any way. He described the feeling as a person would use a rod of electricity to shock an animal to force it to move. Sometimes my husband would wrestle aimlessly for exhausting hours trying to get the thing to leave him alone. When it did leave, it was only temporary!

This spiritual battle was on until Jesus set us free! Another day was still ahead of us! Every night the turmoil was there. The relentless battle was on. It seemed like the enemy was winning! We were at our wit's end as to what to do about this situation. The turmoil was wearing on our souls after all these twenty-one years. Still, as far as we knew, no answer was in sight, but we kept on searching. Little did we know, God was busy working in our behalf!

After one Saturday night of battle for my husband, he had to get up and go to work the next morning at Lee Way Motor Freight in Oklahoma City. There he met his new partner, Mike Messel, for a trip to the East coast. As they approached the Tulsa Turnpike, Mike noticed that Oscar seemed to be upset. He asked him if he could be of any help. Oscar shared that what he had been going through, he didn't believe anyone could help him. So far that had been the way that it was. But Mike didn't agree with him.

Mike told him that he was a born-again, Spirit-filled Christian, and he had the answer we had hoped for all these years! Can you not see this divine plan of God happening here? Our pleas, our hopes, and our answer were on the way and it was being manifested right then and there! For over a year Mike did not work on Sundays! He told the Lord that he did not want to miss Pastor Scheaffer's preaching of the Word of God at Crossroads Cathedral, but God spoke to his heart that there was someone who needed him. In obedience, Mike went to work instead of to church!

My husband then started sharing our problems with him. Sometime later, Mike said, "Oscar, I sense by the Holy Spirit that you are under a satanic attack and we're pulling this rig over right now and casting the devils out in the name of Jesus Christ of Nazareth."

They prayed and Oscar, with the confession of his mouth and believing in his heart, received Jesus as his personal Lord and Savior! He said that he felt a heavy burden lift off of his shoulders. Then he asked Mike if he would go to our home and pray for me because now he knew that I needed Jesus." Mike said that he would as soon as they returned home from the trip.

A few hours later, Mike called me long distance and told me that Oscar had just gotten saved. Of course, since I didn't know what it meant to be saved, I said, "Saved from what?" We then had a thirty-minute discussion on salvation, but being strong in my religion, I couldn't believe any of it. I then said, "If it helped his situation, I suppose it is good." Wow! Was I full of religious spirits!

Several days later, my husband returned home. He shared with me that he had bought a Bible on the road, and in his spare time of not driving, he read the Bible. Even when he was supposed to be sleeping in the bunk, he was reading. He brought home several books for me to read concerning the Jehovah's Witnesses, but I would not read them because I would only read the Watchtower Society's publications.

Oscar asked me if I would sit down with him and read the Bible. I told him I would, but I didn't understand it. He told me that he invited his partner, Mike, and another brother in the faith, Ken Shahan, to come to our home to pray for me and to anoint our house.

Since I had asked several times for the Witnesses to come and pray for us and they wouldn't do it, it was agreeable with me because I wanted and needed prayer very much. This much I knew.

I noticed such a remarkable change in Oscar. He wasn't yelling and cursing me anymore. The neighbors two acres away could hear us before, but it wasn't happening anymore! Unbelievable! He was chasing me around the house to read the Bible with him when before he wouldn't even pick it up!

He wasn't the same person anymore. He was born again of the Spirit of God. He seemed so peaceable and loving. God truly moved in his life. This was God's divine timing and plan for his salvation and deliverance. Without the trip with Mike which God set up, Oscar may not have gotten saved and asked for help for me. Only when he was saved were his eyes opened to see that I needed Jesus. He didn't say that I needed a doctor, a lawyer, a merchant, or a chief. He said, "Emma needs Jesus!"

Chapter 11

MY DELIVERANCE

A couple of days later, Mike and Ken, who didn't even know me, rode their motorcycles over a hundred miles to pray for me.

As they approached our corner, turning from the highway onto the dirt road, Mike heard a strong voice tell him to leave this area, for this was the territory of the one speaking! Knowing the voice was satanic, he was more determined to come and pray for us. When they arrived at our house, Oscar invited them to come in. Mike wanted to pray for me first, which was fine with me. Afterwards, he wanted to pray for the family and walk our land, praying as he went. This really sounded good to me. Bring it on! It was about time, don't you think?

As he laid his hand on my forehead, both men started praying and Mike, with the power, authority, and anointing of Almighty God, commanded Satan to come out of me in the name of Jesus! I stood there thinking to myself, *I don't have any demons in me!* But all of a sudden, I fell down right on my living room floor. I didn't know what was happening to me at that time. All I knew was I was twisting and turning my body, foaming at the mouth, and saying strange words I had never spoken before. They both knelt down beside me and continued praying, "In the name of **Jesus**, come out of her. We plead the blood of Jesus over her. Leave her now and never come back!"

I don't know how much time passed, but they continued praying, not giving up. All of a sudden, it felt like energy came out of my body from the top of my head to the bottom of my feet. A body of energy lifted and totally left me lifeless. I felt I had no strength. I just laid there. They continued praying. Then they lifted me up and put me in a chair.

A few minutes later, I started getting really sick. They continued battling for me in prayer. Within seconds, the sickness left and a peace came into me that I had never known before. Something changed me. It was a drastic change! I looked at my husband and I didn't hate him anymore! I just wanted to be near him. I felt so different. God had delivered me from that demonic possession by using the brothers in faith of the Lord Jesus Christ.

Mike prayed for one of our children who was at home at that time, then both brothers started walking through the house, anointing it with oil and praying and commanding all evil forces on our property to leave and never come back in the name of Jesus. Mike walked around our land speaking the oracles of God, and taking authority against all principalities of darkness that had flooded our lives. We all went outside the house and as Mike walked up to us, we noticed a large whirlwind gathered in the dirt driveway and swirled down the country road and disappeared. It looked like a small tornado of dirt! Glory to God! We knew the evil forces had left!

Because of the faithfulness of the brethren who loved God so much, they wanted to see God set us free. They were willing to risk their lives for us, to bring us out of this bondage we were in. Oh, how grateful we are to them even this day, some twenty-three years later. It is still fresh on my heart what God did through them. We thank God every day for His mercy and grace that carried us through the years of these horrible experiences.

I don't believe Mike or Ken considered the danger they were put in by coming against Satan's assignments. All they knew was they had to obey God and trust Him for their safety. But as they rode their motorcycles home, while crossing a bridge, a rock flew up as a car passed Mike on the highway and hit him in the face. He lost control of his motorcycle and landed on the highway with his bike on top of him. Another car almost hit him, but, praise God, he didn't get hurt badly and there was little damage to his motorcycle. He then gave God praise for protecting him. We found this out days later. It really showed me the love of Jesus Christ through others. Mike and Ken risked their lives to save us!

I thank God for the many people who stood in intercession, praying for me to receive salvation, the free gift of God. I couldn't believe people who didn't even know me or about me would take time to pray for me, but they did! At my mom's funeral, a cousin of ours told me, "Emma Lou, we have been praying for you and your mother for years to get saved." God heard the prayers that were prayed for us and He answered them. But, dear one, it was in God's timing! Immediately after my husband got saved, he, too, requested prayer for me from many church brethren. Even at the truck stop chapels! God is so faithful to perform His Word. He wants no man to perish, but to have everlasting life, and that included me!

Chapter 12

MY GLORIOUS SALVATION AND BAPTISM OF THE HOLY SPIRIT

God wasn't through with me yet! He then sent my neighbor, Zedna, and her son, Wayne, to come and visit with me. They are of the Pentecostal faith. She brought with her several translations of the Bible that we might compare different passages of Scripture. In looking through the *King James Version, The American Standard, The New International,* and the *Watchtower New World Translation,* to my surprise, the Watchtower Bible was different – the only one that added words and deleted sentences, which changed the meaning of the context. For example, John 1:1 says, **"In the beginning was the Word, the Word was with God and the Word was God."** The Jehovah Witnesses' Bible says, **"and the Word was a god,"** meaning that Jesus was a created god, taking away His sovereign deity. I didn't have any understanding of why we were taught this. I always had a lot of questions about the Jehovah Witness doctrine that went unanswered.

Zedna said to me, "Emma Lou, you have been searching for the truth all of the years I have known you." Wayne then looked up at me from sitting at the dining room table, and said, "Emma, do you want to get saved?" I hesitated for a moment, because I didn't know what "getting saved" meant. "Saved from what? Hell?As a Jehovah Witness we didn't believe in hell!"

Then Zedna said, "Emma, would you repent of all of your sins right now and accept Jesus Christ as your Lord and Savior?" I told her that I really didn't know anything about Jesus, but I didn't have anything against Him, so I reckoned I would! So with her leading me in the "sinner's prayer," I repented, confessed with my mouth Jesus as my Lord and Savior, and I asked Him to come into my heart and save me. And He did just that! I believe even quicker than I asked, He came into my life and saved my rotten soul. He saved me from an eternal damnation, death passed over me, and a new life came into me. I now had eternal life – eternal life with Jesus and God forever. He took away all my ugly sins and washed me clean by His precious blood, and threw my sins into the sea of forgetfulness. He will never throw my sins at me ever. Was God through with me now? No! There was more to come!

After my confession of salvation, I felt so warm inside of me I could not hold back the tears. Something inside of me was drastically changed. There was such peace, joy, and love that I had never felt before. Wayne again spoke up and said, "Emma, the Holy Spirit wants you to speak!" I said, "He does what?" All my life I had been taught that speaking in tongues was of the devil. Now, what should I do? Nothing seemed to be the answer because so many wonderful things had happened to me in the past few weeks and months. I am one who will not shut the door on this move!

Then Wayne said, "Raise your hands and say, 'Jesus, I love You.'" I did, but nothing happened, so then he said "Say, 'Hallelujah.'" All the time he was talking to me, Zedna was praying in tongues. About that time, another neighbor, Sue, came in. She too put her hands on me and started praying. Suddenly, as I said, "Hallelujah," I felt a sensation rise up out of my stomach and into my throat and I just let it out! I was speaking in some Chinese language, or that's what it sounded like. I just started crying and speaking in this beautiful oriental language.

I received what the Bible calls "the Baptism of the Holy Spirit and fire." Glory to God! It's wonderful, exuberant, vivacious, absolutely vibrant! I don't know how else to explain this precious moment to you. Zedna encouraged me to continue praying in that heavenly language and assured me that it was the Holy Spirit speaking through me. I didn't know what to do or think. It was so new to me, but inside of me, I was bursting with a tremendous acceleration of joy unspeakable and full of glory.

After they all left, I still could not contain myself. I ran to the bedroom and knelt down on the floor and I cried out to the Lord: "Jesus, if this is You, I want it, but if it is the devil, I don't, because I've had him too long, and I don't want him in my life anymore." Instantly, I started praying more reverently in the Spirit and I didn't stop praying for hours. It was such a wonderful feeling that I had never ever felt before.

I had such a renewing of strength, love, and joy that I had never experienced in my life. I couldn't believe what had just happened to me! It was out of this world! It didn't cost me a dime, and I wasn't high on drugs. All it cost me was giving my whole life, my heart, to God to take care of. I felt like I was on Cloud 9. Even though I didn't know what I was saying, it was so wonderful, I didn't care. I knew that it was from God, and I knew that it was good! The Scriptures say that "all good things come from heaven above," and I believe it!

For many years before I got saved and filled with the Holy Spirit, I had a fear of speaking in tongues. On one occasion at the Kingdom Hall, one of the elders was testifying that a Chinese man he knew was standing next to a Christian who began speaking in tongues while praying. He prayed in a Chinese language. The Chinese man understood the entire prayer and said that it was demonic and it blasphemed Jehovah. So upon hearing this report, I never ever wanted to speak in tongues and blaspheme my Father.

Strangely enough, before we were saved, one of my sons, Tony, went to a Pentecostal church with my neighbors to see a Christian movie called "Left Behind." The movie touched him in such a way that when they got back to Zedna's house, Tony wanted to visit with them for a while as friends do. Suddenly, Mike, Zedna's son, said to her, "Mom, Tony wants to ask you something!" Usually teenage boys want to spend the night with each other's family. Zedna thought this was the issue, and said, "Oh." But Mike said to her "Mom, Tony wants to get saved!"

At that request, Zedna and her family went into the living room, knelt down, and she led him to Jesus! My son received Jesus as his Lord and Savior and then he received the Baptism of the Holy Spirit with the evidence of speaking in other tongues.

When he came back home, he asked me what I thought about people speaking in tongues. I hesitated before I answered because I didn't really know how to answer him. I told him that all my life I was taught that it was not of God, but I would not say because I didn't know for sure. To tell you the truth, I wanted what he had! He was different! He had the glory of God shining around him and a joy in him I had never seen before. I was jealous of what he had and I wanted that experience, but I didn't know how to receive such a blessing.

But now, glory to God, I have that light (Jesus is the Light) and living water (the Holy Spirit) in me also! I am filled with the beautiful Holy Spirit, and I don't have any fear of Him. He will only come into you _if_ you first accept Jesus Christ as your Lord and Savior.

The Holy Spirit comes to you no other way. If you speak in other tongues (I'm not speaking about other languages you can learn), supernaturally speaking, without Jesus in your life, I would tend to believe that it is not of God! All you would have to do then is repent to God for all of your sins and ask Jesus to forgive you and come into your heart and save you. You are then a candidate for another infilling – the Baptism of the Holy Spirit!

Chapter 13

Becoming an Intercessor

Since I had received this wonderful gift from God and had no teaching on the subject, my question was, "What do I do with this?"

Would you believe that God heard me speak this and He answered me?

One of my sons worked in a small town near where we lived and one of his co-workers was having a Bible study in his home. He told my son that if he or any of his family wanted to come, we were welcome. He didn't have to tell me twice. I wanted to learn more about Jesus, so several of the children and I went.

During the meeting, the young man played the guitar and we all sang some beautiful gospel music. As we were singing, he stopped and said to me, "Emma, the Holy Spirit told me to tell you that He wants you to be an intercessor." I said, "What is an intercessor?" He replied that God wanted me to pray continuously for others even though I didn't know or understand what I was saying. I eagerly responded, "I can do that!" Being filled with the Holy Spirit with the evidence of speaking in other tongues, I can pray all day long without hesitation or reservation because I'm praying the perfect will of God for other people's lives and situations.

He led me in the Bible to many scriptures concerning praying in the Spirit. Romans 8:26-27 reads:

> **Likewise the Spirit also helpeth our infirmities: for we know not what we should pray for as we ought: but the Spirit itself maketh intercession for us with groanings which cannot be uttered.**

And he that searcheth the hearts knoweth what is the mind of the Spirit, because he maketh inter-cession for the saints according to the will of God.

Since that night and now knowing the truth, I have truly exercised this gift of God in praying for others as He gives me the unction. I praise God that He entrusted me with this gift, because I never knew how or what to pray for anyone, let alone myself! Now, I can pray the perfect will of God and not pray amiss. I thank the Lord for continuing to guide me in His path.

You might ask, is every Christian called to intercession? I would say "yes," because the Word of God says in 2 Corinthians 5:18-19:

And all things are of God, who hath reconciled us to himself by Jesus Christ, and hath given to us the ministry of reconciliation;

To wit, that God was in Christ, reconciling the world unto himself, not imputing their trespasses unto them; and hath committed unto us the word of reconciliation.

This means reconciling people to God, bringing those to God who are lost, away from Him, and in need of Him. It is doing exactly what an intercessor does – going before God on behalf of others. Every Christian has that opportunity.

In 1 Timothy 2:1, Paul gives a general but strong command to the Body of Christ: **"I exhort therefore, that, first of all, supplications, prayers, intercessions, and giving of thanks, be made for all men."** I believe we should all heed this responsibility to pray.

Jesus came to earth as an intercessor. From the day He was filled with the Holy Spirit until the present day, He has been involved in the ministry of intercession. Romans 8:34 says, **"Who is he that condemneth? It is Christ that died, yea rather, that is risen again, who is even at the right hand of God, who also maketh intercession for us."** Isn't it wonderful to know that Jesus Christ is right now interceding for us? He is our Mediator, a go-between to meet with in order to converse on behalf of others' needs rather than our own, then seeing the one for whom you have prayed walk in victory.

Late one evening after supper, my family was in the living room watching television while I was washing the dishes in the kitchen. All of a sudden, an unction of the Holy Spirit came over me. I felt so grieved, I began to pray and cry. I cried and cried, even though I didn't know why I was crying, but I continued praying in tongues until the Holy Spirit stopped using my voice.

My husband came running into the kitchen, and said, "What's wrong? Why are you crying?" I told him I didn't know what the problem or the situation was. All I knew was I needed to take time and be obedient to pray for someone in trouble. My husband then said, "Why don't you ask God what you were praying about?" I told him that it did not bother me not to know what I was praying because I knew it was God's perfect will. He said, "Ask Him anyway!" So, I did!

Scripture does say to pray that you may interpret, so I asked God for the interpretation. I believe the Holy Spirit said that a man was on his death bed and because I took time to intercede for him, death passed over him at that time. Also, I would be fully rewarded for my obedience! This ended the controversy with my husband! Thank You, Jesus!

Another special time of intercession was when a neighbor came over to our house wanting me to pray with them for their daughter who was in trouble. We sat down at the kitchen table, opened the Bible to different passages of scripture that would encourage and strengthen them, read them aloud, and then began to pray.

We prayed together in agreement because God's Word says in Matthew 18:18-20 NKJV:

"Assuredly, I say to you, whatever you bind on earth will be bound in heaven, and whatever you loose on earth will be loosed in heaven.

"Again, I say to you that if two of you agree on earth concerning anything that they ask, it will be done for them by My Father in heaven.

"For where two or three are gathered together in My name, I am there in the midst of them."

As we were praying, I prayed in the Spirit. All of a sudden, in a vision I saw a semi-truck jackknifed on an Interstate. In another frame, I saw many wooden caskets, all different sizes, lined up against a wall. All of them had a spray of flowers on the top of them. Death spoke out, loud and clear to me! My husband had been an over-the-road trucker for over twenty years at that time, and he was back East driving somewhere.

As we finished praying for the need of the daughter, I said, "Please wait. This is what God has showed me in a vision while we were in prayer." I relayed the vision to them and said, "We need to intercede for Oscar. He is in trouble!" So we joined hands again, and began to pray and intercede. We continued praying until we all stopped at once. It was over! God heard our prayers and answered us! We didn't know when the answer was coming, but we knew God would be faithful to answer us! God also gave me a tremendous peace and I didn't have to worry about it anymore. It was taken care of at that point!

Two days later, the phone rang and it was my husband. He was panting because he had just run several miles to a filling station to use the telephone. No cell phones at that time! He said, "Honey, you won't believe what just happened!" I said, "Oh, yeah? What happened?" "Well," he replied, "I was driving 65 miles an hour down the Interstate and all of a sudden my air hose popped off. I didn't know how in the world I was going to get the truck stopped! But, you know, I got it pulled off on the shoulder and we didn't even have an accident! Isn't that great?"

"Oh, yes," I said! "By the way, were there cars around you?" He answered, "Sure there were!" It was in the middle of the day in town! Then I told him what the Holy Spirit had showed me two days earlier and how we had interceded for him and his partner so they wouldn't be killed or anyone else killed. So we both gave thanks to the Lord for watching over them and protecting them through the power of prayer. He was anxious to get back to the truck and tell his partner the good news of what God had done for them.

I truly value the powerful, anointed gift of the Baptism of the Holy Spirit, to be able to be and do what God has called me to. I thank God that He has entrusted me with His gift and that I may use it for His glory.

Chapter 14

UNFORESEEN BLESSINGS

Even though I was saved and filled with the Holy Spirit, evil was still in our house, and we were still in a financial nightmare. We decided to auction the inventory from the store and close down. About a month later, a group of men came to the store and held the auction. We didn't even take groceries home, because we thought we would get more money at the auction.

To our surprise, thousands of dollars of merchandise and equipment were auctioned off for a little of nothing. I felt sick. With all of our groceries, meat boxes, and appliances, we ended up with $2,650.00! We took that small amount of money and paid an existing bill for gasoline and groceries we had previously purchased. It didn't even leave us enough to buy groceries for our own use!

We were so disappointed and depressed, we didn't know what to do. The following morning, my friend Sue came over to visit me to see how I was. I explained to her about our situation and she calmly sat and listened. She said, "Emma, you know, I was lying in bed this morning and this voice told me, 'Go and see Emma.'" That was the main reason she came to visit me.

She listened to me as I continued pouring my burdens out to her. (At that time, I still didn't know how to put my trust in God enough to pour my burdens on Him.) After a while, without much comment, Sue left. I was glad she had come to visit me. It showed me that she cared and it lifted me up.

Hours later in the evening, Sue and her husband drove up in the driveway. I called for them from the porch and told them to get out and come in the house. I shared that we didn't have any food to offer them, but we could sit and talk a while. She replied, "We can't stay long, but we have something for you!" She told me to come out to her car, so I walked to her car and, lo and behold, it was full of groceries! Her husband opened the trunk and it was full, too! She said, "Emma, it's all for you!" I said, "No, it will be all right. It will work out someway!" Then my husband came out of the house, and hearing the conversation, he said, "Yes, we'll take them and thank you very much!" I just stood there and cried. She laughed and hugged me and said it was from her church. She also handed me $85.00 in cash and told me God wanted to bless us.

I didn't know how to receive it! While we were in the store, we would help people in need with groceries or gasoline if they had no way of paying for it, especially if they had children, but never did we think we would get a return on our giving. They unloaded their car and brought the groceries in the house and sat them on the 8-foot table, bench, and floor. I sincerely believe there was enough food to last several months.

The extraordinary thing about it was that we had only attended their church, Ted Holloway's Fellowship, a couple of times. Today, I still testify about the love that congregation showed us. The Jehovah Witnesses said that they bought us. Yes, they did. I agree with them. But they bought us with love! It was not a selfish intent to get us to come to their church. It was an offering of love to someone in need. After all, doesn't the Lord say to feed the hungry? Not only does this mean spiritually, but it means physically too.

A couple of weeks later, Sue came again to visit me and asked if I wanted to go to another ladies' meeting to learn more about the Holy Spirit, and of course, I said "yes." After we got there, we worshipped the Lord in song and then the Word of the Lord went forth. I was so hungry to hear all this good news about Jesus and the Holy Spirit that I had never been taught. It was all new stuff to me. I was like a pig at the food trough, just getting fuller and fuller. It was so wonderful. I had such peace, love, joy, and liberty that I had never known before. The Bible says, **"Therefore if the Son makes you free, you shall be free indeed"** (John 8:36 NKJV).

Chapter 15

NO MORE FEAR

It seemed like things were turning around at the Hernandez house, but the evil presence hadn't left yet! My husband and I and all of our children were saved, but I needed to do one more thing before I had total victory in my life. As I was at the women's meeting, after the service was over, it was asked if anyone needed prayer. I went forward and told the Christian sister about the evil still in my house. She said, "Would you like to repeat the sinner's prayer over again?" I said "yes." She began the prayer and I repeated it as she spoke it. I believed in my heart what I was confessing with my mouth:

"Heavenly Father, I come to you a sinner. I'm sorry for the way I have lived. Jesus, I know that You are the Son of the Living God, that You died for me, You were resurrected, and You now sit at the right hand of the Father. I ask You to forgive me of all of my sins, in my thoughts, words, and deeds. Jesus, cleanse me with Your precious blood of all unrighteousness, iniquity, and transgressions. I denounce and renounce Satan, witchcraft, magic, fortune-tellers, voodoo, and any other evil force from Satan's kingdom. I break all curses, hexes, and vexes that have ever been spoken against me and my family from past generations, in the name of Jesus Christ of Nazareth. Jesus, I ask You to come into my heart today and save me. Live in me. I confess You with my mouth and believe in my heart that You are God's Son. I accept You as my Lord and Savior. I thank You, Jesus, for saving me. Right now I am a child of God and I'm on my way to heaven!

If you prayed that prayer with me, and believed in your heart what you prayed, you too are born again (saved). God has forgiven you of all of your sins just as you have asked Him, so receive your miracle!

After I prayed that prayer, I started praying in tongues. (A person cannot speak in tongues of the Holy Spirit unless he or she is born again.) I broke out in a sweat. In a vision, while I was praying, I saw a baby being born. I knew this baby was me. All of the ladies just reverenced the moving of the Holy Spirit in that place. When I stopped praying, I felt like a new person. Truly, God had taken me into another dimension of the Spirit. I was actually born again when my neighbor, Zedna Moore, led me to Jesus months earlier. But this time, I took authority over all the works of the demons and satanic powers by renouncing Satan and his kingdom. By accepting Jesus as my Lord and Savior and His shed blood, I felt so clean, pure, and innocent because I was a new babe in Christ. I didn't feel dirty anymore. At that point, I was totally delivered from the spirit of demonic oppression. Death passed me over and eternal life that only Jesus can give came into me!

The teacher remarked that the Lord had given her a scripture for me in Zechariah 3:1-6 and that I was as Joshua was:

And he shewed me Joshua the high priest standing before the angel of the Lord, and Satan standing at his right hand to resist him.

And the Lord said unto Satan, The Lord rebuke thee, O Satan; even the Lord that hath chosen Jerusalem rebuke thee: is not this a brand plucked out of the fire?

Verses 1-2

I felt in my heart that God had pulled me out of the fire and had given me a whole new beginning. When I arrived home, I knew I needed to do some housecleaning. So being led by the Holy Spirit, I started searching for every *Watchtower, Awake,* and every publication, including the Bibles from the Watchtower and Tract Society, I had accumulated for over thirty-three years. I looked in my cellar, closet, under the beds, in the garage, etc. and put them in one big pile. I threw them into the fireplace and burned every one of them! What a joy that was! The literature from the Watchtower and Tract Society were like idols to me. I had put my trust in those idols instead of the true and living God. I had boxes and boxes of them all over the house, inside and out, *but no more!* Halleluiah!

That same night, for the first time in twenty-three years, I went into my bedroom, undressed, climbed into bed, and laid my head on my pillow. In the darkness, I looked around the room and to my surprise, there was the most beautiful, wonderful peace I had never felt in my life. I give total glory to God for performing this miracle in my life.

There were no more people, eyes, or faces staring at me. No heads (without bodies), no skulls, no animals jumping out at me, and nothing attacking my body. I tell you, *there was no more evil in my house! The curse of witchcraft, of which we were all victims, was broken by the power of Jesus, in His name and by the power of His shed blood!* There was a sweet-smelling aroma in that room. It was so beautiful! I laid there and cried *tears of joy!* No one on this earth had the answer for us to get out of that horrible situation that almost took our lives. Jesus alone was the Answer!

Now I can shout it from the rooftops, "You don't have to live in fear anymore! Jesus is your Answer!" When I accepted Jesus as my Lord and Savior, renounced anything to do with Satan and his kingdom, accepted the atonement of Jesus' shed blood at Calvary, burned all the idols, then *all the fear that I had for over twenty-one years totally left me!*

I would be lying if I told you that nothing else ever occurred again over the years, but I can truthfully tell you, I do not walk in fear anymore. Now I have faith in the Word of God. God has given me power, authority, Jesus' shed blood, the name of Jesus, and His Word to use against any enemy that tries to attack or to bring fear against me or my loved ones. In Jesus' name, I can bind, rebuke, and cast out any demons and command them to leave us, get out of my house, and get off of my land. They are trespassing on God's property! Without a doubt in my heart, they have to leave! And as Jesus said to them, NEVER COME BACK! Within seconds, they are gone! Praise God!

I found out that I cannot fight the evil spirits with my natural being. This is a spiritual battle, and it must be won in the spirit realm. This is where the Word of God comes in. Jesus came to destroy the works of the devil. It was because of my lack of knowledge that I was almost destroyed. The Bible says, **"My people are destroyed for lack of knowledge . . ."** (Hosea 4:6). I wish I would have read the Bible for myself and believed it instead of listening to what other people taught or believed. The Bible says, **"Let God be true, but every man a liar. . ."** (Romans 3:4).

Any more attacks are not on a regular basis, for I know Satan got the message. Now he tries to come in other areas. I believe as long as I am alive and serving the Lord Jesus Christ, I will still be on the devil's most wanted list. But Jesus took all that *fear* from me, and I will continue to exercise the authority against my enemies in the name of Jesus. I still say, "Greater is He who is in me, than he who is in the world!" (See 1 John 4:4.)

It keeps me on my toes and in the Word of God and in prayer constantly. But I continue to thank God every day for all that He has done for me, what He is doing now, and what He is going to do in the days ahead. I come to Him daily with thanksgiving and praise.

After twenty-three years of Satan's harassment, it is so wonderful to be able to lay my head down on a pillow at night and go to sleep without fear. If I cry, it's because of the goodness, mercy, and grace of God that He has given to me. The Bible says that Jesus is **"the way, the truth, and the life. . ."** (John 14:6). Truly He is!

A few weeks later, Pete invited me to go to his church. I agreed and I met him the following Sunday. At the end of the service, the pastor asked if anyone needed prayer for healing or anything. I went to the altar and stood in front of the platform where he stood. He had never seen me before, and I didn't know him either. He took one look at me and declared, "Sister, the

Holy Spirit has revealed to me that you have had a curse of witchcraft on you, but **as of this night, there will never be another curse put on you. Jesus has set you totally free of all curses!** Glory to God! Needless to say, the power of God came over me and I was slain in the Spirit, which means I fell backward on the floor under the power of God. I rose up off of the floor with a new hope in my life. God spoke to me through the pastor that I would never have to face that dilemma again in my life. (If a curse of witchcraft tried to come on me, it would <u>not</u> prevail.) Now it was shouting time! Victory is mine! Glory to God!

Now, do you think God left us in that horrible financial bondage we got ourselves into? The answer is no! Here again, God moved His mighty arm in our behalf! Ten years earlier, we had purchased a ten-acre property for $16,500.00. We remodeled the small home, made it larger, put on brick siding, and sold it for $57,500.00. We paid all existing bills, paid cash for the home we lived in for twenty-one years, and we were totally debt free! God truly moved again in our behalf and delivered us!

After God so miraculously saved, healed, and delivered me out of the hand of Satan, you might think that part of my life is a closed book. Now I want to use my past as a stepping-stone to higher elevations with Christ, as a testimony of what Jesus can and will do in people's lives so we can give Him glory. There is a purpose and a plan for everything that He does, and Jesus is no respecter of persons.

Chapter 16

EVANGELIZING

My past is no longer a stumbling block for me. I desired so much to learn about Jesus and what He says in His Word, that God helped me to attend two years of Bible college and graduate. I went to church, revivals, tent meetings, and crusades. Every time the door was open, I was there. I was so hungry to hear the Word of God, to learn to know Jesus for who He is, and to fellowship with the saints.

If you are wondering about the title of this book, *Tears of Joy,* what would bring forth those tears? God gives us joy unspeakable and full of glory! What a joy it is to be a witness for the Lord Jesus Christ and to share in the joy of His salvation. To be able to portray Jesus Christ, the True and Living God, in truth and unconditional love inside of me, gives me such peace, joy, and love that I had never experienced before. I couldn't convey to others what I didn't have myself, and that is *the genuine love of God.* I had a form of godliness, but I denied the power thereof. I pushed my religion onto my family, friends, and other people at the doors of their homes. There was no hope in the memorized passages that I spoke. It was religion and religion kills!

For years now, God has done exploits through me. When He healed me, I believed that He could heal everyone! With that kind of compassion of Christ within me, it compelled me to go into the highways and byways, grocery stores, thrift stores, garage sales, gas stations, prisons, nursing homes, truck stops, hospitals, you name it. I wanted to go there. One missionary from Mexico told me "Adelante, Emma!" That means, "Go forth!"

The joy of my salvation, what God brought me out of, and where He is taking me compel me, with compassion, to **go and tell the wonderful works that God has done in my life!** Jesus is alive and He is still saving, healing, delivering, restoring, and performing miracles.

Wherever I am, I walk up to people and ask if I can pray for them. Most of them say "yes," and when I lay my hands on them, I can feel God's healing virtue leave me and go into them. You can see by their countenance that the power of God is touching them. There is such a peace that comes over them, it's really unexplainable. But when they open their eyes, the joy of the Lord is on their faces, and they say, "The pain is gone!" Glory to God! What can you say to that? I get so energized, I want to lay hands on every sick person I come in contact with!

You might be wondering, *Is this scriptural?* James 5:13-16 NKJV says:

"Is anyone among you suffering? Let him pray. Is anyone cheerful? Let him sing psalms. Is anyone among you sick? Let him call for the elders of the church, and let them pray over him, anointing him with oil in the name of the Lord. And the prayer of faith will save the sick, and the Lord will raise him up. And if he has committed sins, he will be forgiven.

"Confess your trespasses to one another, and pray for one another, that you may be healed. The effective, fervent prayer of a righteous man avails much."

Jesus says in John 14:12 NKJV, **"Greater works than these he will do, because I go to My Father."** I believe the Word of God and in obedience to His Word, I step out in faith and let God do His glorious works in others through me for His glory!

I continue praying for wisdom concerning prayer for others I do not know but come in contact with. Not everyone wants to be healed for one reason or another. If you were disabled and drawing a pension, then when you get healed you might have to go back to work! Some people believe like I did years ago that healing was done away with when the apostles died. Therefore, they don't want you to pray for them. I believe they miss out on receiving miracles God has for them. But even Jesus couldn't do any mighty miracles in some places because of unbelief. So I just continue trying to be led by the Holy Spirit to show me who to pray for and when to pray for them.

The most wonderful thing about praying for people is not so much for the healings or miracles, but it's when I see a real conversion from a person praying the sinner's prayer with me. By the power of God, they are changed and brought out of darkness into the glorious light of the Lord Jesus Christ. No words can really describe the glory that surrounds this person. What an experience it is to behold the glory, for from their eyes *tears of joy* flow down their cheeks. A beautiful smile comes forth, replacing a face of sadness and oppression.

There is nothing on this earth that can give you the warmth, comfort, and feeling of acceptance as when you ask Jesus to come into your heart and you accept the sacrifice He made on the cross for you and me and the world! Wealth, health, and prosperity in this lifetime cannot bring you the instant gratification that only God can.

When I prayed for people as I met them in my path, at first I didn't use wisdom. I didn't have enough of God's Word in me to know what, when, or even how to do what He wanted me to. I think I had a double portion of zeal. I didn't want anything to hold me back because I thought it was God's perfect will! I was sure listening to voices that I thought were God! Even your own thoughts can get you in trouble!

One day in a grocery store, I noticed a man with a cast on his leg from the top of his thigh down to his ankle. He was standing in the aisle, leaning on crutches, and looking at canned goods. This voice spoke to me and told me to go over to the man, lay my hand on him, and say, "In the name of Jesus, be healed!" Thinking it was the Lord speaking to me, I obeyed! I had no fear! I walked up to the man, slapped him on the shoulder, and said, "Be healed in the name of Jesus!" I calmly took off with my cart going down the aisle, not looking back. All of a sudden, I heard a loud crash of cans hit the floor. I was afraid to look back to see what had happened! I have chosen not to do that anymore!

I've learned over the years to wait upon the Holy Spirit to tell me when, and even then, sometimes I wait too long to move. I repent if I have missed the Lord, and He gives me second chances! God is so good to me! Sometimes if it sounds too good to be true, it's probably not God. I say to God, "Is this really You?" This is a learning process, but I do know He does lead us, especially by His peace. It's wonderful to pray for a person and see a miracle happen and in your presence they give glory to God. It's awesome to behold the glory on their face.

I may never be like Healing Evangelist Oral Roberts or some well-known evangelist, nor reach millions of people, but God has used me to touch people on a one-on-one basis. But regardless, God only expects out of us fulfillment of the plan He has for us. No more and no less. We all have a different measure of talents He wants us to use for His glory, and He will prepare and equip us for that ministry. But whether our outreach is large or small, it is such a joy to see one more person plucked out of hell and from the clutches of Satan!

I have found that everywhere I go, there are people who need prayer. I believe when Jesus healed the five thousand, five thousand were healed! I'm not the One who heals anyway. It is God, and as I have found out, it's in His timing, not mine! I'm just a vessel who God uses to do His will in this earth. Then, I give Him all the glory and praise for what He does.

On another occasion, I had gone to the grocery store, and as I walked down the aisle, I noticed an elderly lady. She was dragging her right leg, tightly holding on to a walker, and headed toward the meat section. A voice spoke to me and said, "I want you to go over and speak with her!" Believing this was the Lord,

I said, "But Lord, I don't know what to say! She may not want to listen to me!" Again, He spoke to me and said, "Go, and I will give you the words to speak!" Then, I walked boldly up to her and struck up a conversation. I asked her several questions and made a few statements before I asked her what happened to make her leg stiff. I asked if she'd had a stroke. She replied that she had been in an auto accident two years earlier, and it damaged her hip and leg. Stiffness had resulted after she went through surgery.

Then, I started telling her about the sickness that I had for over twenty-one years and how Jesus healed me in a matter of seconds. She then said, "I know Jesus can heal me. I have had many prayers prayed for me, and God has promised me that someday He will heal me!" All of a sudden, it rose up in me to tell her, **"This is your day! God wants to heal you today!** God is going to set you free! May I pray for you? God has sent me here today!"

She looked up at me with such joy in her face and with the faith of God in her heart. Believing God had spoken to her through me, she said, "Yes, in the name of Jesus, you can pray for me!"

Then, I took out a small bottle of anointing oil and anointed her head and began to pray for the healing virtue of God, in the name of Jesus, to go into her and make her whole again. Within seconds, she started moving her right foot, then the leg, and then from the hip down, she started swinging her leg back and forth and dancing right in the aisle. People looked at us and quickly turned down the other aisles. She was crying and screaming, "Thank You, Jesus! Thank You, Jesus!" I stood there in awe at what God had just done! I just rejoiced with her! This was truly the first miracle I had ever seen in which Jesus used me.

I didn't know what else to do after this experience, but to praise God and thank Him for what He had done for her. Then, I told her I needed to go on with my shopping, since I had done what the Lord wanted me to do. We exchanged names and phone numbers and I went on.

About fifteen minutes later, I was walking down another aisle and I saw her walking without her walker! I thought to myself, *My God, where is her walker?* As I went closer, I saw that it was in the cart she was pushing. She didn't need it anymore! She had received from God His promise of healing. I tell you, my heart leaped for joy, and I burst out into tears. It was indeed a joy to see the power of God move instantly to heal this woman of faith. I left the store feeling ten feet tall and praising God. I was blessed, too, by being obedient to what God told me to do, even though I was afraid at first. With faith in God, I overcame fear and His will was accomplished!

Throughout the years, I have laid my hands on many people. God has truly shown me that He is the God of love, mercy, compassion, and justice. He has touched lives of others, even in my immediate family. I thank God for the ministry He has given to me.

There were two special people in my life that God touched through me – my mom and my dad. I want to relate the experiences in this book to show you again that God's Word is truth, and He is faithful to His promises to us. Perhaps this may help you to believe, not only for your own salvation, but also for your lost loved ones. Acts 16:31 says, **"And they said, Believe on the Lord Jesus Christ, and thou shalt be saved, <u>and thy house</u>."**

After I got saved, it was like a fire was shut up in my bones, to go and tell my friends and relatives everything God had done for me. I wanted them to experience the love, peace, and joy I had experienced. I wanted them saved, filled with the Spirit of the Living God, and serving Him with all of their heart, mind, soul, and strength!

You might say this started my first missionary journey! Perhaps your own immediate family is your missions ground where God wants you to work before you take off to South America. Start where you are! Cultivate that ground, plow it up, plant lots of good seeds of love, and let God do the growing!

Chapter 17

TESTIMONY OF THE MIRACULOUS SALVATION OF MY FATHER

One afternoon I went to visit my dad, who lived with his two sisters in Oklahoma City. He had been divorced from his second wife for about fifteen years. As I shared my testimony with him, he listened and received what I was saying from the Lord. Later, I asked him if he would say the sinner's prayer with me, and he said "yes"! He repented of his sins, asked God to forgive him, and received Jesus Christ as His Lord and Savior. Then, I prayed for his physical body and left. I praised God for my dad's salvation, knowing that when he died, he would go to be with Jesus in heaven.

Since we lived fifty miles away, I didn't see him on a regular basis. He was very active for his age. He had played the guitar for over sixty years, and he had a school of Hawaiian music. He was in several bands over the years, and he was the lead guitarist in the Senior Citizens Band in Oklahoma City. The group went to many places to play music for different organizations. He always desired to go to Hawaii, and before he died, God gave him the desire of his heart.

My dad at almost eighty years old, had been having several light heart attacks throughout the years. He spent a week or so at the hospital, but he was released and given another appointment for a later date.

Periodically I would go to visit Dad and my aunts. At this particular visit, Dad was not at home and my Aunt Mary didn't know where he was. We went back home, saddened that we didn't get to visit with him.

The following morning, I got a call from Aunt Mary saying that Dad was in the hospital. Fluid was filling his lungs. I wanted to go to be with him since I was his eldest daughter, but with my husband being unemployed at that time, we didn't make too many extra trips to the city unless it was absolutely necessary!

I was so moved in my spirit that I knew I needed to go to be with my dad. I sought the Lord in prayer as to what to do. In my spirit, God told me to go see Zedna, my neighbor. I didn't know why at the time, but I obeyed Him. She is a preacher of the gospel of the Lord Jesus Christ and really has the faith to touch God in heaven through prayer. I knew that about her, so I went quickly to her home at the end of the road.

As I entered her home, I began telling her about my dad. I told her the situation of our finances. Without hesitation, she went into her bedroom, got her purse, and handed me $20.00! She said, " I believe God wants you to go to be with your dad!" She hugged me and I thanked her for the love offering. I ran back home and got ready to go to the city.

As I entered the room in the Intensive Care Unit at Baptist Memorial Hospital, a nurse looked at me and said, "You must be Emma! Your dad has been saying all day long that Emma was coming to be with him! I said, "Yes, I am Emma, and I will be staying with him as long as it takes!"

Dad started telling me he was pleased with the doctors. They were running tests on him to find the reason why his lungs continued to fill up, causing heart attacks and choking.

He said, "Honey, will you stay with me?" I told him I would and I laid my hands on him and prayed. Then, I told him to rest for a while and I was going to go to the waiting room, but I would check on him periodically. He thanked me for coming and praying for him. He wanted to bless me financially for making the trip, but I told him the Lord had already taken care of it. Just being there with him was blessing enough for me. He grinned at me and said that he was going to turn over and rest a while. Then I could come back in the room to be with him. I kissed him on the cheek and walked out of the room to go to the waiting room.

As I sat down in the chair, only minutes passed when I heard, "Code blue. Code blue." I watched as doctors and nurses went running down the hallway, pushing machines as they went. I didn't know what was happening because I hadn't been in a situation like this before. I only remember seeing situations like this on television, but this was for real! Someone needed emergency care and it was my dad!

Minutes later, a young nurse and another woman came hurriedly into the waiting room and walked over to me. My eyes were focused on these women as they approached me. I just sat there in amazement, not knowing what was going on.

Finally, the young nurse, crying, said. "I don't know what happened to your dad. He just turned over and died! You need to get hold of your family members because he may only have an hour or so to live. The doctors have shocked him with the paddles and brought him back to life, but he is in a coma state."

I was stunned! I just sat there for a moment not knowing what to do or say. I couldn't even think straight! Suddenly, a situation was upon me that I had never experienced before. I've heard about these things happening, but I didn't think it would happen to me!

Finally, I got a grip on myself and ran to the telephone and started calling the family. When my eldest brother arrived, we went into the Intensive Care Unit to be with Dad. He just lay there, staring at the ceiling. He was breathing very heavily and holding his breath, which seemed like a minute or two, then letting it out! He continued this type of breathing. The doctor said that his heart was fibrillating. All of his vital signs were failing. He didn't expect my dad to live much longer. It was just a matter of time. But what the doctor didn't say was that it was in God's time!

Hours and days passed, and doctors said that he was stable. No better, no worse. But I never left Dad's side for the next several days. They moved him into another room, and I sat in a chair across the room from his bed, read my Bible and prayed.

One afternoon as I sat beside him, he lifted his arm into the air, made a fist, and started swinging it in the air, as if he was in a boxing match. The look of terror seized his face. He turned his face from one side to the other from the pillow. He twisted his head back and forth and slung his arm into the air, attacking something that he feared with all the power he had within him. I saw nothing in the natural, but having been in this type of situation myself (trying to fight evil spirits), I was not ignorant of what was happening to my dad.

A nurse entered the room and stood beside him and watched as he was fighting his battle. She said, "Well, he is fighting something!"

At that point, enough was enough! Anger rose up in me for the devil to harass my dad when he wasn't able to defend himself. I rose from my chair with the power and authority that God had given me, and I spoke these words, **"Satan, I bind you and your tormenting spirits and cast you out of this room and away from my dad, in the name of Jesus Christ of Nazareth!"**

All of a sudden, after I prayed that prayer of deliverance, my dad's facial expression changed to the look of peace and his arm dropped to his side on the bed.

The nurse quickly said, "I have got to go now and check on some other patients!" I don't think she realized what had happened in this supernatural experience with my dad. I sure am glad I was there to help him and that God gave me the gift and calling on my life to be a witness for Him and to manifest His goodness and glory to others. I thank God that He heard my prayer and answered it.

Five days later, Dad's condition was the same. He neither moved anymore nor spoke. His eyes just stared at the ceiling. He still had the irregular breathing, rapid heartbeat, his kidneys were failing, but for some unknown purpose, he was hanging on to life!

By this time all of my family members were at the hospital. Then, I decided to go home and rest and let the others stay with Dad. I had a peace about leaving.

Very early at the quake of dawn on Sunday morning, as I lay in my bed, suddenly I awoke and started praising the Lord. Immediately, I heard a voice say to me, **"This is resurrection day!"** I said, "Yes, Lord, I know it is!" It was Easter! I started praying more. During the time of prayer, the Lord showed me a vision of things to come. It's as if I was watching television. In this vision, I saw all of my family gathered around my dad, holding hands and praying for him. I told the Lord, "Okay, I'll do it!" I got up, dressed, fasted the morning meal, prayed, and left for church.

After receiving salvation, I never returned to the Kingdom Hall of Jehovah's Witnesses. From what I had heard from other relatives who were Jehovah Witnesses, I had been disfellowshiped from the congregation. Letters were sent to the three congregations in different areas I had attended, stating that I was a wicked servant and they were not allowed to fellowship with me (which meant "don't eat with her, speak to her, or visit her, under any circumstances"). Only an elder could communicate with me.

About a month after I had left the congregation I attended, an elder called me and wanted to have a meeting with me and two other elders. I told him, "No, but I am going to do more for you than you have ever done for me." He answered, "And what is that?" Out of my mouth came a revelation of God that I had never spoken in my life! I told him that I would pray for them to come out of the darkness and come into the glorious light of the Lord Jesus Christ! I probably don't have to tell you, he hung up!

Would you believe, all of this happened because I became a "born-again Christian"? But glory to God, I praise God anyway!

Later, it was rumored, "The devil healed Emma and that is why she left the society!"

My Bible (I prefer the *King James Version*) doesn't tell me that the wonderful miracles, raising the dead, casting out of devils, cleansing the lepers, and healings of sickness and diseases have anything to do with the power of the devil! My Bible says that these things happen through the power of Jesus Christ! In fact, Jesus came to destroy the works of Satan! (See 1 John 3:8.)

Now and then, I attend a nondenominational church. Upon arrival at the church that I had attended for many years, I asked for special prayer for my dad, and told them of the vision I saw and what the Lord told me to do. Since they know I'm radical for Jesus, many brethren believed me and said that they would be in intercession for me during this time.

After the church service, I drove to the hospital. I walked up to the head nurse in ICU. I didn't know if she was a Christian or not, but boldness came over me and I told her that the Lord had spoken to me and told me to say a prayer of resurrection over my dad. I stood steadfast in my belief that God was going to raise him up and heal him, or take him home that very day! I was immovable in what I believed.

I didn't know what direction God was going to move, but I told the nurse that I needed all of my family to pray with me for this miracle to happen. The nurse looked me in the eyes, and said sternly, "You've got it!"

Then, I turned and walked into the room where Dad was laying. About eight people were already there and silence came as I entered the room.

I began to speak with boldness the instructions that the Lord had told me to do and that I didn't know how to pray this prayer in English, because I didn't know what or how I ought to pray for this miracle. I needed to pray in tongues (the gift of the Holy Spirit). I knew I would pray the perfect will of God and not pray amiss.

In gentleness and love, I asked that anyone who did not believe in what I was going to do, to go into the waiting room until the prayer was finished. I wanted the Holy Spirit to move. Two of the brothers-in-law left the room.

I asked the remaining family members to gather around Dad's bed with hands held together. My sister said all she wanted was God's will be done in his life. I agreed with her!

I got my anointing oil from my purse and told Dad that I was going to anoint him for prayer. He didn't respond, but I knew it was all right! I poured the oil all over my dad's head until it ran down his head, and then I took the hand of my husband and laid my right hand on Dad's forehead and began to pray.

I looked up to heaven in the name of Jesus and started praying in the Spirit. I started weeping and crying aloud, travailing in my spirit. I knew I was doing warfare in the spirit for my dad. During this time of prayer, God revealed another vision to me.

This time I saw myself inside of a courtroom. I was the lawyer who was pleading my dad's case to the Judge. I felt in my spirit that I was asking God to have mercy on my dad because I knew God loved him and wanted him to live and not die. This is the perfect will of the Father, because John 3:16 says, **"For God so loved the world** [that includes my dad], **that he gave his only begotten Son, that whosoever believeth in him should not perish, but have everlasting life."** A few years earlier, I had led my dad to the Lord. He had accepted Jesus as his Lord and Savior.

I continued praying, tearfully, until the Holy Spirit stopped. I just stood there and waited on the Lord to tell me what to do next! All of a sudden, I started singing the most beautiful praise song to the Lord for what I knew He was going to do for my dad. Even though I didn't know what I was singing, the song brought tremendous peace with it.

After I finished singing, it was as if a whole bucket of heat was poured over me from the top of my head to the soles of my feet. I knew, beyond a shadow of a doubt, that something good was about to happen.

We then released each other's hold and began to leave the room. I didn't feel in my spirit to take hold of Dad and say, "Get up, Dad. You're healed!" I just had to trust God to do whatever He was going to do. This work was done in the spirit realm. Now, I just had to wait on the outcome or the manifestation of the answer to our prayer.

My husband suggested that we go back home since there were so many there to be near Dad, but I said, "No way!" I knew something good was about to happen, and I wanted to be there when it happened.

I did agree to go and sleep in our van in the hospital parking lot that same night rather than curl up in a chair again. I had been there all week long with Dad. A good night's rest would probably do me some good.

Early next morning, we went back into the hospital. As we were walking down the hallway, the doctor met us and started exclaiming, "I don't know what happened! I don't know what happened!" I asked him, "What are you talking about?" He said, "It's your dad! He's sitting up in bed, talking up a blue streak! We haven't given him any different medicine than we have all week long! I don't understand it!" I started praising the Lord! I told the doctor, "Jesus told me that He was going to raise him up and He did it, just like He said He would!" God healed him, that's what happened!

I hurriedly ran to Dad's room and there he was, sitting up in the bed, talking and talking, just like the doctor said. I just cried and said, "Thank You, Jesus! Thank You, Jesus!"

I went over to Dad's bed, leaned over him, hugged and kissed him. I couldn't stop praising the Lord! I was told that late Sunday night Dad came out of the coma. By morning, he was ready for breakfast. During the night, the nurses had been giving him juice and water, but what was astounding to the doctors was that everything in his body was functioning perfectly! Only God could have done such a miracle.

Dad reached out, took my hand, and said to me, "Honey, why did I go through a tube?" I told him that I didn't know. My husband asked him, "Dad, did you go all the way through it?" Dad said he didn't know. I asked him, "Did you see Jesus or the glory of God? Did you see the streets of gold?" He said, "No. Where I went, it was only white! Nothing but white!" But, with a little hesitation, he said, "But I played with two angels. Honey, they were huge! They had great big wings and they wore white robes!" I asked him if he played the guitar with them, but he said "no." He said that they just danced around.

At that point, he started jerking his body around to demonstrate how they danced. Then he said, "Honey, they shoved me back to earth! They shoved me back to earth!" I said, "Dad, why did they send you back?" Quietly he said, "Well, Honey, maybe it wasn't my time to go or maybe I'd better change my way of living!"

Right then, the Spirit of God rose up in me and told me to pray the prayer of repentance with Dad. I moved closer to him and asked, "Dad, would you pray with me and repent of your sins and ask Jesus to forgive you for the way you have lived?" He said, "Yes, Honey, I will! Yes, Honey, I will!"

Then, I asked Dad to repeat the prayer after me and believe in his heart every word he spoke. He agreed and I started praying. I was having Dad repeat so much of God's Word in that particular prayer that my husband spoke up and said that I didn't have to make him quote the whole Bible!

But in my heart, I wanted to make sure if God called him again that he would not just go where it was white or halfway! I wanted him to go all the way through those pearly gates to be with Jesus forever! If I had anything to do with it, I wasn't going to risk the chance of him missing heaven. After the time of prayer, a great peace came over me and I released him back to God.

I felt in my heart that God had brought him back for a purpose. One, another daughter had flown in from Texas to be with Dad. She had spoken to me and said she was blessed to spend some quality time alone with him, and in that time there was a healing of hurt relationships due to a lot of misunderstanding. Neither had seen nor heard from each other in over five years. After they talked and got things out in the open, both of them received the love they needed from each other. Through many tears, they were able to embrace each other, and say, "I'm sorry. Will you forgive me?" A peace came over both of them which they hadn't had in years. Another brother thought Dad lived a thousand miles away. Therefore, he hadn't been in touch with Dad for years. Good came from that also. God is so good! What Satan means for evil, God turns it around for good for His glory!

As issues in hearts and minds were settled, later that evening Dad's physical condition reversed. Every sickness or ailment that was previously in his body the week before the miracle, returned.

Two days later, my eldest brother and I were at the hospital early in the morning to visit Dad. His physical condition was steadily growing worse. He could hardly speak, but this time he didn't have any fear in his eyes. A peace surrounded him.

The nurse came in and brought him some orange juice. He took a sip of it and said, "The next time that I come to the hospital, I'll bring my own sugar!" He was laughing, of course, when he said this! Those were his last words!

The nurse came in and asked us to leave the room so she could turn him over and change the sheets. So we stepped out, just a few feet from the room. All of a sudden, screams of "Code blue" rang out again! Doctors and nurses went running into Dad's room with machines and shocked him again. Once again, he had turned over and died!

The doctor came out to us and said that we needed to make a fast decision on whether or not to put Dad on a respirator or to let him go. They couldn't continue shocking him, because it would damage his heart even more. I knew in my heart that

God had brought him back to life so he could repent of his ways and be prepared for heaven. But since my brother was older, I told him to make the decision and I would be in agreement with him. He said, "Let Dad go home! He's ready!"

The doctor told us that we could visit him for the last time. It would probably be only a matter of minutes before he would pass. As we entered the room, he was tilted upside down a little, then he had one more attack. I called out to him and said, "Daddy, don't be afraid. Jesus is with you!" He didn't respond. It was over. I knew he was with Jesus because the Bible says, **"To be absent from the body** [is] **to be present with the Lord"** (2 Corinthians 5:8).

Through this, I saw a loving, compassionate, merciful God, who, in His divine nature, honored our prayers of intercession and was faithful to perform His Word that He wanted no one to perish.

My heavenly Father saved our dad from an eternal hell, damnation, and total separation from Him. You might say, "I thought you had led your dad in the prayer of salvation prior to his hospitalization and his death experience." That is true, but I didn't know about his comings or goings since we lived miles apart. Later, after his passing, the legacy he left behind showed me that he had not been living a Christian life, even though he was a good person! Being good won't get you to heaven, and he himself recognized his need to change his way of living and repent of his sins.

I thank the Holy Spirit for giving me the unction to pray the sinner's prayer with Dad. God knows all things and reveals them to us to do His will on this earth. There is no sin in heaven. So by God's grace, mercy, love, and honoring His Word above His name, He brought my dad back to life. He gave Dad another chance to get things right with Him so he could go home with a clean slate. I give God praise for His lovingkindness.

Chapter 18

TESTIMONY OF THE MIRACULOUS SALVATION OF MY MOTHER

Another special person in my life was my mom. She was truly liked and loved by many people, but she didn't have a personal relationship with Jesus because of her religion.

As years passed and she was unable to participate in the "field service" or attending many of the meetings, conventions, etc., she was disfellowshiped from the congregation of Jehovah Witnesses, with whom she had been involved for over forty years (with different congregations throughout Oklahoma). Even so, she was still dedicated to the cause. Nothing would move her spiritually. She was spiritually blind, just as I had been!

After I got saved, she, too, denounced me and turned away from me and my family for over seven years. I tried to talk with her about Jesus and what a difference He had made in my life, but she didn't agree with me. I only angered her because she was very strong in her belief. All I could do was pray for her and continue to walk in love toward her. After all, she was still my mother.

I can't say it didn't hurt, because it did, but standing in faith and in God's Word, I trusted that someday, somehow, she too would be saved. I got to the point of saying, "Lord, whatever it takes, save her soul!" When you make a statement like that, you had better be ready for whatever takes place!

My mom loved to play bingo. I would tell her not to play it, because I felt that it was a form of gambling and I don't think Christians should gamble. That is my opinion! But she was very dedicated to do whatever she put her mind to do.

Several times a week, she played bingo. The thing of it was, she won frequently, sometimes a lot of money, and with it she would help others in need of finances. Sometimes she helped us with $20.00 to buy us groceries when we were in some hard times.

One particular night, I heard she had won a sizeable amount of money, because she had won at bingo four times in a row. She got so excited, she had a stroke and a brain hemorrhage in the bingo parlor! She was taken by ambulance to ICU at Hillcrest Hospital in Oklahoma City, Oklahoma. I didn't know this and no one called me!

The next day, my spirit was grieved and the Holy Spirit told me to go to Oklahoma City to see a couple of prayer partners named Myrtle and Myrtle Lou. Both of these precious women of God really knew how to pray and go into the very throne room of God. (God had used Myrtle Lou to witness to me before I got saved.) She was a little four foot, eleven inch, grey-haired grandma, passing out gospel tracts in a Thrift Store. Not only did she give me a tract about the impending rapture of all the Christians, she prayed for me right there in the store! Imagine that! She was truly a big part in my Christian walk when I first became born again.

Back to Mom's story! Listening to the Holy Spirit, I went to Myrtle Lou's house not really knowing what was taking place, but that I needed to go to pray with others of like faith. Upon arriving at her house, she said, "I will call Myrtle also because she is a mighty prayer warrior and a preacher." I told her that would be great! There is power in numbers! Scriptures say that one can put a thousand to flight, two can put ten thousand to flight. (See Deuteronomy 32:30.) Praise God! I knew I needed help in prayer!

When Myrtle arrived a few minutes later, I told both of them why I had come. I had felt so grieved in my spirit and had a heavy burden, but I didn't know why or for whom. So they said, "Let's pray and intercede and maybe God will reveal to us what's going on!"

After an hour or two of prayer, I rose up and said, "I need to go to the Blind Thrift Store!" This is the store I went to nearly every week for ministry and clothing for my family. My mom went there quite frequently also. So I went thinking I might see my mom there.

As I entered the store, I looked around, but I didn't see anyone I knew, and my mom wasn't there either. So I said, "Okay, Holy Spirit, I'm here! What do You want me to do?"

Suddenly, the phone rang and the manager spoke out, "Is there an Emma Hernandez in here?" I was astounded, because no one knew I was there but my prayer partners! Immediately I went to the counter and took the call. It was one of my brothers calling me. He told me about Mom and that I needed to get to the hospital as soon as possible. I asked him how he knew I was there, and he said, "Something just told me to call the Blind Thrift Store!"

Then I hurried to the hospital and went to ICU. I went to the nurses' station, and they directed me to my mom's room. I walked over to her and asked her if she knew who I was. Slowly she said "yes." I said, "Mama, will you repent of your sins right now and ask Jesus to come into your heart and save you?" She answered "yes," again very slowly because it took all the effort she had just to say that much! But I knew this was the most important thing to do in her life while she was still alive. After she dies, and stands before God, not having repented of her lifestyle and sins, it's too late! God says, "Now is the time of salvation!" Neither she nor I knew if she had a tomorrow!

So believing this with all of my heart, I said, "Mama, just repeat this prayer after me." Then, I said, "Heavenly Father," but she couldn't respond. Her brain was swelling and perhaps that was too much for her to have to say at that point. I told her to listen to the words, believe with her heart, and think the words with her mind, and God would acknowledge her prayer of faith. This is one prayer He will listen to because it is His perfect will. God gives each and every person on this earth a measure of faith to pray and accept Him as Lord and Savior!

Then, I repeated the prayer of salvation with Mom. I asked her afterwards, "Mom, are you saved? Did you ask Jesus to come into your heart and forgive you of your sins?" Slowly, she said "yes." Glory to God! My mom was now ready to go to heaven if this was what God wanted, by that simple prayer of faith in the True and Living God. Even though I didn't know what was going to happen to her, a great peace came over me.

Later, the doctor told some of the family who were there in the hospital that if he didn't operate on her brain, the bleeding would continue and she would die. It was a 50/50 deal. We had to make this decision for her, but knowing she had received Jesus, who is eternal life, I knew God was with her now and I didn't need to worry about the outcome. She was in the Master's hands. God says, **"I will never leave thee, nor forsake thee"** (Hebrews 13:5). Fear left me concerning her life! After the family talked it over, we decided she needed to have the surgery.

The next day, they moved her to another hospital where the surgery would be performed. All of the family was there, hoping and praying that all would go well.

After many hours of waiting, finally a doctor came out and told us that it was over and she would soon be moved to recovery. Minutes later, they brought her from the operating room down the corridor. We walked up to her as they were moving her into the recovery room, when she spoke out with a loud voice: "I want to go home. I want to go home." The voice was very deep, speaking with much authority. She looked up at the ceiling, pointed with her finger, and said, "Do you see that? They are recording me. They are thieves. They are after my money." This did not sound like my mother! It scared me. Her eyes were glassy and her expression was different than I had ever seen before. A cold feeling came over me.

Immediately I left her and went to the nearest telephone booth. I called Myrtle Lou and told her I thought something evil had entered into my mom. I knew it was not my mother speaking! I knew it was an evil spirit speaking through her!

Myrtle Lou told me not to be afraid, but to go to my mother, anoint her with anointing oil, pray for her, and cast the devil out! She assured me that she would get hold of Myrtle and they would both be in prayer for me. She reminded me that God has given us the power over the enemy! Luke 10:19 says, **"Behold, I give unto you power to tread on serpents and scorpions, and over all the power of the enemy: and nothing shall by any means hurt you."**

God's power is available to you and me if we just have the faith to believe it and exercise that faith. God will enable us to do what we need to do through Jesus Christ. All I needed to do was release my faith and draw on God's power to set Mom free!

Myrtle was a preacher, and when she spoke, the anointing fell. So right there in the phone booth we prayed and I was encouraged about my mom. I agreed to do what she told me to, and I was not afraid of what I had to do, regardless of what others would think! I knew God was with me. Sometimes we just have to step out into the water, knowing beyond a shadow of doubt God is leading us! It may be scary, but as Mary told Jesus' disciples, **"Whatsoever he saith unto you, do it"** (John 2:5). Just do it!

I went back to the waiting room and sat down, prayed silently, and waited. (Sometimes we need to wait on the Lord to make sure of His perfect timing.) We were told that only two at a time could go in to see her. So my brother Russell and my uncle went into the room to see her first. They weren't gone but a few minutes when they came back into the waiting room with their heads hanging low. The look on their faces showed much oppression. My uncle said, "Well, you have a mother, but I don't know if you'll want her!"

They sat down beside me and started telling me what Mom had said. She had humiliated them. She told her own brother that he was not her brother and he wasn't anything but a "bald-headed so-and-so." Then, she turned to her own son and declared he wasn't her son, he was just a kinky-haired _____. Bad! Neither one could hold the tears back. Now I knew what God had revealed to me was true!

Russell, my brother, looked at me, and said, "Emma, it's your turn. Are you ready for this?" I said, "Yes, I am." Of course, he didn't know what God had in store for Mama. As I got up to go into the room to be with Mom, my Aunt Bill decided to take her turn with me, which was okay, because she too was a Christian. But all of a sudden, my adopted sister decided to go with us.

I didn't think it would pose a problem, but had I known what was going to transpire in that room, I would have gone alone. I was going to do a work for the Lord and the devil didn't like it! I had a check in my spirit that my adopted sister shouldn't go with us, but I didn't know what to say to her, so I just let it go.

As we walked into the room, I went up close to Mom's head. Aunt Bill went to the other side of the bed, and my sister was at the foot. I asked Mom how she was. She said, in a very deep voice, "Look up there!" (She pointed to the ceiling at a water sprinkler!) "They have a recorder and they are listening to everything we are saying. They want to steal my money. They are nothing but liars."

By this time, I knew I had to pray the prayer of faith and bring deliverance to Mom. So I said, "Mom, I'm going to pray for you. Okay?" She agreed. Then, I took a small bottle of anointing oil that I carry with me, and I anointed her head. I laid my hand on her forehead, and in the name of Jesus Christ of Nazareth, with all the power and authority God has given me, I began to bind those evil spirits and command them to come out of her and never come back again.

I have learned over the years, you do not cast out devils, except you bind them first. In Matthew 18:18-20 NKJV it says:

"Assuredly, I say to you, whatever you bind on earth will be bound in heaven, and whatever you loose on earth will be loosed in heaven.

"Again I say to you that if two of you agree on earth concerning anything that they ask, it will be done for them by My Father in heaven.

"For where two or three are gathered together in My name, I am there in the midst of them."

I spoke with such power and authority that seconds later, my sister let out screams. She was so frightened she ran out of the room to go and get my brother. I don't know what she told him, but he went to get the head nurse outside Mom's room, and told her to get me out of there! "Look what she is doing to my mom!" he said.

At that time, my brother was not saved, so he didn't understand what was happening in the spirit realm nor the authority I was taking. I could see the nurse headed my way. I didn't give up praying because of fear of what she would say, because Mom needed help and God was using me to do it! As the nurse threw back the curtains and walked in, I was praying these words: "And devil, you will not curse these nurses, doctors, or this hospital anymore! In fact, I command you to shut up your foul mouth and never speak again, because you're coming out in the name of Jesus and never return!"

The nurse bowed her head and stood in reverence while I continued in prayer. All of a sudden, looking at Mom's face, her mouth closed tighter than a drum! Glory to God! It was over! The battle was won! Victory was in sight! Now, it was time for Mom to rest a while!

We left Mom's room and went back to the waiting room. As I walked in, everyone looked like they were praying. Their heads were all hanging down. No one could look me in the face. Finally, one of my brothers came over to me and said, "Didn't I tell you that Mom is not your religion?" I said, "I know, but I had to obey God!" He said, "Just what did you do in there?" I told him that in the name of Jesus, I cast the devils out of her!

His face just drew a blank! He didn't know what to say, so he went and sat down! No one said anything else to me. That was okay, too, because they didn't know God's Word either or they would have understood! Have you ever felt alone in a room full of people? I sure did! But, glory to God. I knew God was doing a miracle in Mom. So I didn't let feelings get in my way. I refused to get offended by my family because of their lack of spiritual understanding!

Now it was time for round two! After a while, my uncle and Russell went in again to see Mom, but this time the look on their faces when they returned to the waiting room had changed! The oppression had left! God was working in everyone, not just Mom! She wasn't quite so bad now. They noticed a change in her. I knew God would do a quick work in her! I didn't go in any more. I just sat there and prayed. That night, everyone left but my brother, his wife, and me. We spent the night at the hospital.

Early in the next morning, I left to go to the truck stop to pick up my husband who had just come in from a long trip across country. Then, we went back to the hospital, and we were the first ones of the family to visit Mom.

As we entered her room, there was an awesome glow around her. It was as if the glory of God shone round about her. Her face glowed with such a beautiful peace. Never had I seen her so beautiful! She had such a sweet spirit in her. She spoke so soft and gentle. I knew beyond a shadow of a doubt that God had cleansed her of all demonic possession from the top of her head to the soles of her feet. It was so wonderful to see her like that. I had never seen Mom this way before. It was indeed a miracle.

She commented to Oscar how good-looking he was with his new cowboy hat! Oscar said to me, "Ask her to say the sinner's prayer with you again out loud. Tell her you want to hear it." I said, "But I believe she's saved!" "I know," he said, "but ask anyway!" So I said, "Mom, will you pray with me again out loud?" She said, "Yes, Emma, I will!" Then we all prayed together. She looked up at me and said, "Emma, I'm saved and I'm not afraid to die!" You see, long ago she had told my cousin she was afraid to die. Now, praise God, with Jesus in her heart, she wasn't afraid to die anymore! She was free of the fear of death. She had life in Christ Jesus now.

A few minutes later, Oscar went into the waiting room while I visited Mom alone. There were things in my heart that needed to be said. I had been told for years that Mom hated me and didn't love me. I carried this burden around for years and it was so heavy for me. It weighed me down, because I needed her love. So I said, "Mama, I want to ask you to forgive me for anything I have said or done to offend you, because I love you very much. But Mama, I cannot go back to being a Jehovah Witness because I love Jesus so much! He has saved me and done so much for me. I know it's the truth!"

She looked up at me, took my hand, and said, "Emma, I have always loved you. You should not have listened to that person!" Again, when I obeyed the Holy Spirit when He told me to go to Mom and ask for forgiveness, even though I didn't feel I was guilty of anything, I was set free of that burden. A joy came over me because I believed what she spoke to me. I knew she was sincere! It was just her and me in the room. She had no reason to lie to me. Her countenance and her words spoke truth. Now I had a peace. I could let her go of the hurt I had for years.

God says in His Word in Mark 11:25-26 NKJV:

"And whenever you stand praying, if you have anything against anyone, forgive him, that your Father in heaven may also forgive you your trespasses.

But if you do not forgive, neither will your Father in heaven forgive your trespasses.

I thank God, because the Word of God is truth. It will set you free when you obey it! Now, Mom didn't tell me to go back to the

Witnesses like she had previously. Now she was saying that Jesus was going to heal her. What Mom didn't know was that Jesus had healed her over two thousand years ago when He went to the cross!

First Peter 2:24 NKJV says, **"Who Himself bore our sins in His own body on the tree, that we, having died to sins, might live for righteousness – by whose stripes you were healed."** Isaiah 53:5 NKJV says, **"But He was wounded for our transgressions, He was bruised for our iniquities; the chastisement for our peace was upon Him, and by His stripes we are healed."** Regardless of what others say, healing is for today, just as it was then.

Mom started telling the doctors and nurses about Jesus! When my uncle and aunt came to see her, they couldn't believe the change! They knew God had touched her. Everyone, even unbelievers, knew there was a miraculous change in her.

A few weeks later, something happened in her brain, and she wasn't the same anymore. She had no control over her own mind, and different voices or personalities spoke through her. She began screaming all night, not even realizing what she was doing. I spent the night with her one time and as she screamed, I prayed and read the Word of God throughout the night.

The next morning when the nurses came in, they asked what happened to her, because she wasn't screaming. I told them that I prayed and read to her out of the Bible. One nurse replied that they did everything they could, but not that! I left the television on Channel 14, Trinity Broadcasting Network, twenty-four hours a day, to help Mom hear the Word of God, to help her in her spiritual walk with the Lord, and to bring life and healing to her body!

Months passed and the doctors could do no more for her, so I took her to our home to take care of her myself. She was paralyzed on her right side from the stroke. I have to admit, it was extremely hard to care for her and my family as well. We had five children at that time. My husband was always on the road, and a lot of times I could have used his help in lifting her 165 pounds onto the hospital bed. I constantly had to put her on the potty-chair and into the wheelchair. I was smaller in stature than my mom and it was a bit of a struggle for me, but I sure learned to lean on Jesus for my strength to help her.

After just a short period of time, her physical condition worsened and I had to return her to the hospital. Several people in the family made fun of me and said they knew that I couldn't take care of her, but the doctor said in front of the entire family that for me to try to take care of her was admirable because it was better to try and fail than to fail to try! No one else said anything after that.

The doctors put Mom in a rest home a few days later, but that didn't work either. When I wasn't there to read to her and pray with her, and she wasn't hearing the Word of God, she still continued to scream all the time at the top of her lungs! No one knew what to do about it! It was driving them bizarre. But soon she caught a staff infection, so she was moved back to the hospital and put in isolation. We had to dress with gowns and masks before we could go in to see her. By this time, she couldn't feed herself, talk, or move any part of her body. But she could hear, and when my Aunt Bill or I would feed her, we would tell her to swallow. She refused to swallow for anyone but us, so one of us had to be there daily to feed her.

One afternoon before I went to see Mom, I went to a prayer meeting with my neighbor at her friend's home. While we were there, the other sister said that the Lord had impressed upon her to take communion. We agreed. She went to get the necessary bread, grape juice, and the Bible so we could start the service.

Before we took communion, we examined ourselves and repented of any and all sins so we did not take the communion unworthily, because the Bible states in 1 Corinthians 11:27-31 NKJV:

Therefore whoever eats this bread or drinks this cup of the Lord in an unworthy manner will be guilty of the body and blood of the Lord.

But let a man examine himself, and so let him eat of the bread and drink of the cup.

For he who eats and drinks in an unworthy manner eats and drinks judgment to himself, not discerning the Lord's body.

For this reason many are weak and sick among you, and many sleep.

For if we would judge ourselves, we would not be judged.

It is the will of God for you to take communion when you are saved. But my mom had never participated in this service because of her religion and the belief that she had to be one of the 144,000 who were going to heaven. She believed she was not one of the chosen. I thank God, He desires that we go to heaven.

Scripture in 1 Corinthians 11:23-26 NKJV states:

For I received from the Lord that which I also delivered to you: that the Lord Jesus on the same night in which He was betrayed took bread;

And when He had given thanks, He broke it and said, "Take, eat; this is My body which is broken for you; do this in remembrance of Me."

In the same manner He also took the cup after supper, saying, "This cup is the new covenant in My blood. This do, as often as you drink it, in remembrance of Me." For as often as you eat this bread and drink this cup, you proclaim the Lord's death till He comes.

During the time of prayer, God showed me in a vision to prepare to have communion with my mom. I leaped for joy with this revelation of what else I could do for her! So after prayer meeting, I went to the grocery store to purchase the necessary elements I needed for communion and went to the hospital.

When I arrived, Aunt Bill was sitting beside Mom. I told her and Mom that I was going to read the Bible about taking communion and I was going to give it to Mom. Aunt Bill said she wanted to take it too. (As of January 7, 2005, my Aunt Bill is in a nursing home and she is 102 years old! God has truly given her long life.)

I started reading the Word of God in 1 Corinthians 11, and when I finished reading a portion of scripture, I told Mom to open her mouth so I could put the cracker (which represents Jesus' body) in it, and I told her to swallow. She did! Then, I read some more scripture and put a teaspoon of juice (which represents Christ's blood) up to my mom's lips and told her to swallow, and she did that! Peace and joy came over me again! I believed God had done another miracle in Mom.

A couple of days later, I returned to the hospital. I was told that all the screaming had stopped! I didn't realize there was healing in taking communion, but God knew! God is so wonderful!

Mom lay there peaceably now, but all the family was ready for her to go to heaven! A family member even told me not to go in and pray for her to be healed on this earth. It was a period of four months now, and they were tired and weary and wanted to see her suffering end.

The doctors warned us that the end was nearing, but I knew it wouldn't really be the end for her. It would be a new beginning. Because of her receiving Jesus as Lord and Savior, she was just going to be translated to heaven to be with God for all eternity. Out of her body of sickness, she was going to a place where there is no sickness, disease, or death.

I had such a peace to let her go, because I knew where she was going! As I looked at her in those last minutes, one little tear fell from her eye. Several of the children surrounded her bed and we said our good-byes and that we loved her. Then she drew her last breath and went home. Truly she received the greatest healing!

Immediately, I began to pray in the Spirit and in a vision, I saw two large angels in white walking across the clouds to take her to that glorious city. I saw her in a little white robe as she walked toward the angels. The scripture came to me at that moment, **"To be absent from the body** [is] **to be present with the Lord"** (See 2 Corinthians 5:8.)

Then, I walked into another room and called the pastors of my church, James and Wanda Frizzell. I told them that my mom had just passed away, and I asked Wanda if she would perform the service. She said, "Of course, Emma. We are your pastors and we are your family. We are here to meet all the needs of you and your family and friends. Whatever you have need of, we're here for you!" She said, "Even now, the Lord is giving me the scripture, **"To be absent from the body is to be present with the Lord!"** It was confirmation to me that Mom was with Jesus. God says in His Word that out of the mouth of two or three witnesses, let a thing be established!

Pastor Wanda said the church would even fix the meal and everything we needed for everyone. I thanked God for my church family and their love.

One hurdle down, another to go. Mother had told my other brother that she wanted a Jehovah Witness funeral (this was before she got saved). I talked with my sister, Glenda, and asked her to pray with me that everyone would be in agreement to have the funeral at my church, Jesus Alive Evangelistic Church, in Newcastle, Oklahoma. I didn't want any arguments or disagreements in this area. Glenda agreed with me.

I went into the waiting room where my other brother was. I knelt down beside him and told him about my church and what my pastors had revealed to me, who were willing to do all that was needed to be done in this situation, but I wanted his approval. I didn't want anyone to be hurt or angry with me. I wanted total agreement! He had lived with Mom for years, and I know he wanted to honor her wishes, but he also knew that she had been disfellowshiped from the Jehovah Witness congregation, and he at that particular time didn't fellowship anywhere in particular. I still wanted peace among the family. He then looked at me, and said, "Emma, you got it!" I just hugged his neck and cried. I knew God was moving in all of us through this situation.

Pastors James and Wanda did as she had spoken. Several Jehovah Witnesses were at the church for the service, and many relatives attended who had not been in church for years. I know that the Holy Spirit moved in all of our lives during that service, because the message that was given was primarily on salvation.

As years have now passed (the funeral was held on April 10, 1987), I have had the privilege of leading several of my relatives to the saving knowledge of the Lord Jesus Christ.

Chapter 19

SALVATION OF MY SISTER, DARLA

In conclusion to this story of what Jesus has done and is doing in and through my life, I want to share one last testimony of a family member.

Darla was a very beautiful young woman. She was married young and had three beautiful children. Before she had the second child, with me being on fire for Jesus, I witnessed to her about Jesus and she accepted Him as her Lord and Savior. We didn't live near each other. Therefore, I didn't get to visit with her except on special occasions.

One day another relative, visiting with her, convinced Darla to move with her to help her with her children and job and other reasons I don't know about. Darla left her own family behind to do this. After a period of six months or more, because of differences, she moved back home. She was shocked when she arrived at her home, because her husband had divorced her for abandonment, and she had no visitation rights of the children. Everything was taken away because of her desertion. This totally devastated her and she did not know which way to turn. Needless to say, the devil was at her door knocking big time and she went into sin city.

The children grew up not knowing their mother. She married again years later and moved to Texas. A loving grandmother raised the children in a godly home and atmosphere.

About seventeen years ago, I went on a missionary trip with fifty people to Monterrey, Mexico. I went with a Baptist Evangelistic Group from Global Missions out of Dallas, Texas. Upon arriving at the hotel, seven of us were moved to another small town called Saltillo. I was one of them, and for some reason, I was not registered at any hotel or motel.

We chose roommates and mine was a Pentecostal like me! I'm not prejudiced, but I do like to be free to pray in the Spirit when I want to! There are some denominations that don't believe the way I do, so God answered my prayer in that respect!

The following morning, Sunday, as we prepared to go to the church services, a grieving spirit came over me and I just wanted to cry. I felt such a heavy burden, but I didn't know what was wrong. I told Sister Zola about the burden I was carrying. She said, "Emma, let's pray until you get a release and peace concerning the issue." We both began to pray, asking God to help me to discern this need.

I thank God for the Baptism of the Holy Spirit because I did not know how to pray concerning this situation! During the time of prayer, I had another vision. It was a cemetery and a casket! I told my roommate, "I see death! But I don't know whether it has already happened or it is going to happen." She said for us to continue praying until we heard from God. Then we went on to church, but for the next three days, I continued in prayer because the burden didn't lift.

Zola suggested that I call home regardless of the cost and find out if anything was wrong, so I did. My husband answered the phone, and said, "Honey, where are you? We've tried to find you for three days. You aren't at that hotel in Monterrey where you are supposed to be. We couldn't find you anywhere!" I told him that seven of us had been moved to Saltillo, but the reason I had called was because I was very troubled in my spirit about something, and I didn't know what had happened.

My husband had some very disturbing news for me. He said that my sister, Darla, had been killed three days earlier. Her husband was driving over a hundred miles an hour on an Interstate, went out of control, and the truck flipped down an embankment and rolled several times. From what I heard, he had his safety belt on, but she didn't. She was thrown out the back window and rolled over fifty feet down the highway, breaking the brain stem of her neck.

My husband told me not to worry about trying to get home because they had already had the funeral. He told me to be careful while I was still in Mexico, and we hung up!

I just sat down on the bed and cried. I knew the lifestyle my sister had chosen. Again, I cried out to the Lord. He said in His Word that it is His will that no one perish and go to hell for an eternity! Also, Acts 16:31 NKJV says, **"Believe on the Lord Jesus Christ, and you will be saved, you and your household."** I said, "God, this is Your Word, and You are faithful to Your Word."

Later that night, when I went to sleep, I had a dream. Darla was hovering over me. She looked so beautiful. A look of peace and glory was all around her and she said to me, "Emma, stop worrying about me. I'm okay!" With a big smile on her face (she looked like Sally Fields, the movie star), she said again, "Emma, thank you for telling me about Jesus!" At that point, she disappeared! I woke up the next morning with such an excitement and joy. God had answered my prayer and gave me such a peace.

I am so grateful to God for His love, which covers a multitude of sins. I knew that I knew that Darla was in heaven with Jesus. No one will ever convince me otherwise, because God gave me that dream, fulfilling the promises in His Word.

You can say that you don't believe in visions and dreams, but I am here to tell you the Bible is truth. Joel 2:28-29,32 NKJV reads:

> **"And it shall come to pass afterward that I will pour out My Spirit on all flesh; your sons and your daughters shall prophesy, your old men shall dream dreams, your young men shall see visions.**

> **"And also on My menservants and on My maidservants I will pour out My Spirit in those days . . .**

"And it shall come to pass that whoever calls on the name of the Lord shall be saved. . . ."

On that particular missions trip, going house to house every day along with other nationals, we were blessed with leading 1,232 souls into the Kingdom of God. Glory to Jesus! It was my first missions trip, and I had the privilege of leading around twenty-seven people to the Lord with my testimony. I said to the Lord, "Next year when I go, give me more souls for the Kingdom of God." He did!

Upon arriving home, my husband told me that Darla had lived two hours in the emergency room. It only takes a minute to repent and get right with God when you do it with all of your heart! I know beyond a shadow of a doubt she was saved! Perhaps when God gave me that unction to pray and intercede for someone, even though I didn't know who the prayer was designated for, God showed mercy upon Darla and saved her. He honors His Word above His own name! (See Psalm 138:2.) Prayer works!

Ecclesiastes 3:1-2 NKJV says, **"To everything there is a season, a time for every purpose under heaven: a time to be born, and a time to die. . . ."** There are other scriptures that say there is an appointed time for man to die, and then the Judgment. I believe when Jesus is in your heart, you never die. Your spirit lives forever, and you just pass through this country into a greater one! That's why Jesus went home to prepare a place for us! Glory to God!

Chapter 20

ENCOURAGEMENT TO EVANGELIZE

What else can I say about this awesome God I love to serve? God has put Mark 16:15-20 NKJV in my heart, a word to all born-again Christians:

> "Go into all the world and preach the gospel to every creature.
>
> "He who believes and is baptized will be saved; but he who does not believe will be condemned.
>
> "And these signs will follow those who believe; In My name they will cast out demons; they will speak with new tongues;
>
> "They will take up serpents; and if they drink anything deadly, it will by no means hurt them; they will lay hands on the sick, and they will recover."
>
> So then, after the Lord had spoken to them, He was received up into heaven, and sat down at the right hand of God.
>
> And they went out and preached everywhere, the Lord working with them and confirming the word through the accompanying signs. Amen.

Your mission field can be in your own home! God first, then your husband, your children, and then your neighbor. You may say, "I don't know what to say or do." The Holy Spirit knows and He is our Helper!

When speaking to someone you don't know, you could ask, "Do you know Jesus loves you?" That wasn't a sermon! But just at the mention of His name, His love can change a broken heart, a grieving spirit, and lift burdens.

For example, I was going down in an elevator in a hospital and had a few floors to go. A woman with her head hung low was standing in the corner. I knew I didn't have much time before I got off, so quickly I said, "Little Lady, do you know how much Jesus loves you?" She looked at me so astounded, surprised that someone who didn't know her would give her any encouragement. She quietly said, "Thank you!" But I didn't stop there. I continued telling her how Jesus says that whatever you go through, He will never leave you or forsake you! She started to cry and said again as the doors opened, "Thank you. I needed that!"

Isaiah 61:1-3 NKJV says:

> **"The Spirit of the Lord God is upon Me, because the Lord has anointed Me to preach good tidings to the poor; He has sent Me to heal the brokenhearted, to proclaim liberty to the captives, and the opening of the prison to those who are bound;**

> **"To proclaim the acceptable year of the Lord, and the day of vengeance of our God; to comfort all who mourn,**

> **"To console those who mourn in Zion, to give them beauty for ashes, the oil of joy for mourning, the garment of praise for the spirit of heaviness; that they may be called trees of righteousness, the planting of the Lord, that He may be glorified."**

God Almighty has called, chosen, anointed, equipped, and filled us with His Holy Spirit to be able to accomplish what He wants each of us to do. Let the Holy Spirit (not anyone else) lead you. You are special in His sight. Through Jesus Christ, you are worthy to do and be what God wants in your life. In Matthew 5:14 NKJV Jesus says, **"You are the light of the world. . . ."** In verse 13 He says, **"You are the salt of the earth. . . ."** So be salty!

Isaiah 60:1-2 NKJV tells us: **"Arise, shine; for your light has come! And the glory of the Lord is risen upon you. For behold, the darkness shall cover the earth, and deep darkness the people; but the Lord will arise over you, and His glory will be seen upon you."**

In John 4:35-38 NKJV Jesus says:

> **"Do you not say, 'There are still four months and then comes the harvest'? Behold, I say to you, lift up your eyes and look at the fields, for they are already white for harvest!**

> **"'And he who reaps receives wages, and gathers fruit for eternal life, that both he who sows and he who reaps may rejoice together.**

> **"'For in this the saying is true: "One sows and another reaps."'**

> **"'I sent you to reap that for which you have not labored; others have labored, and you have entered into their labors.'"**

Today is the day of salvation! My prayer for you today is to take hold of what God has done in my life. Trust Him to provide whatever your need may be, whether it is salvation, healing, deliverance, or restoration. There is nothing impossible with God. If it hasn't happened for you yet, don't give up! Stand on the Word of God as if your life depends on it!

Acts 2:38-39 says:

> **Then Peter said unto them, Repent, and be baptized every one of you in the name of Jesus Christ for the remission of sins, and ye shall receive the gift of the Holy Ghost.**

> **For the promise is unto you, and to your children, and to all that are afar off, even as many as the Lord our God shall call.**

With the baptism of the Holy Ghost, you have the power and boldness to be a witness for Jesus, not counting the other blessings you receive with it. You magnify God, build up your innermost faith, intercede for others, and pray the perfect will of God when you pray in the Spirit. A big plus is that Satan does not know what you are praying when you pray in other tongues (in the Spirit).

It seems to me that the cults have us beat in witnessing. I wish I was wrong, but I do know as a Christian when a couple of us went door-to-door witnessing in a small town, when the people were outside and we approached their property, they ran into their houses and shut the door! They thought we were Jehovah Witnesses. We had to tell them, "We are born-again, Christians!" Then we were allowed to talk to them about Jesus.

We really are the ones with the truth, power, and authority with the name of Jesus, the blood of Jesus, the love of Jesus, the written Word of God, and the angels to help us live and evangelize for Jesus every day!

Where is the dedication of Christians today? God tells me, "Go and tell, Emma." (See Mark 16:15.) I take it literally! Let's show the world that we are the true witnesses of Jesus Christ and the Kingdom of God! Jesus is coming again really soon, and some people in the world have not heard that He came once! I want to take as many souls to heaven with me as I can!

In closing, I want to share Psalm 40:1-4, which speaks to my life and the ministry to which God has called me:

> **I waited patiently for the Lord; and he inclined to me, and heard my cry.**
>
> **He brought me up also out of an horrible pit, out of the miry clay, and set my feet upon a rock, and established my goings.**
>
> **And he hath put a new song in my mouth, even praise unto our God; many shall see it, and fear, and shall trust in the Lord.**

Blessed is that man that maketh the Lord his trust. . . .

I don't shed tears of pain, sorrow, or fear anymore, but *tears of joy!* I have been to the pit of hell, but now I am reaping tears of the joy of Christ in my heart and life.

I cannot relate to you in words the ecstasy that I feel when I have the opportunity to lead someone to Jesus. For when there is a real conversion of that person's life, their countenance changes. Tears begin to flow down their faces, and a joy rises up in them that you just can't explain in words. I want to cry and rejoice with them. I can feel that new life stirring inside of them that screams out, "I'm free, I'm forgiven, I'm not in bondage anymore!"

It's like you want to take off running, dancing, and rejoicing! You want to do something! It's real! It's alive! It's like a new baby being born, innocent, without guilt, condemnation, fear, anger, bitterness, loneliness, shame, or remorse, but oh, so clean. Not dirty anymore! Accepted in the Beloved. Not rejected anymore! When Jesus comes in, He so warms your heart, strengthens you, loves you, comforts you, and lifts you up like no man on this earth can.

I have been in the prison ministry for fourteen years now. It is such a joy and a privilege to serve the Lord in this way. This is where God directed me to go, and whatever or wherever He takes me, I want to do His will. It is His ministry!

For many years, we have had a two-hour service on Sunday at the Lexington A&R ministering to nearly forty different women each week. A lot of the times I go alone (except the Father, Son, and the Holy Ghost are always with me) and I'm not afraid. These are women who need Jesus! After all, sinners are the ones Jesus came to save, and as I minister God's Word to them, Jesus is speaking to my heart, too! Have you heard the song, "God's still working on me"?

Sometimes when I enter the room, I feel a sense of oppression when the women gather together after coming out of their cells. Sometimes they have to stay in lockdown and can't really hear the Word of God. But through prayer, God gives me favor with the guards and they open the doors and let them come out! Before I go to the prison facility, the pastors in my church, Grace Chapel in Lexington, lay their hands on me, anoint me, and send me forth with a prayer covering!

I go expecting God to do miracles in the lives of these women! And glory to God, He does! I begin with prayer, and then we have a beautiful time of praise and worship. Sometimes I take a musical instrument with me and play it, or I take my CD player. Sometimes I play my Jewish tapes, and I teach some of them to dance. Even if we don't get the right steps, they forget they were oppressed! Those devils take off when we glorify Jesus and sing about Jerusalem! After maybe fifteen minutes of dancing, the women who participate are laughing, hugging each other, talking, and just rejoicing. Some tell me, "You did it this time, Reverend Emma!"

Now, they are ready to hear the Word of God! The Holy Spirit has been moving in their lives. The women sit at the edge of their seats, with their eyes fixed on me as I share the word of the Lord. I thank God for the anointing that is upon me to be able to preach the Word of God and share my testimony with them.

Some of them cannot stop the tears from rolling down their faces. Some can relate to what has happened in my life. I am there to give them hope in Jesus Christ – not what I can do for them, but what God Himself can do for them. There is nothing impossible for the Lord if they are willing to surrender to Him.

Truthfully, I never leave that place until I say a sinner's prayer with them. Each time I go, many of the women get saved or rededicate their lives to God. Many of the women experience a real conversion. You can sense it by the expressions on their faces. The glory of God shines on them and through them.

As we pray, miracles and healings happen in their bodies. I anoint them with oil and lay my hands on the sick. In the Bible it says that we shall lay hands on the sick and they shall recover! (See Mark 16:18.) You can see the expression on their faces change when the pain leaves their bodies! They don't know what to say! I tell them to say every day, "Thank You, Jesus!" I tell them to change their confession! "Don't brag on your arthritis anymore! We just gave it back to the devil!"

This is my reward from God for saving me, healing me, delivering me, restoring me, and changing me so I can go and do what He has called me to do. This is why I can't explain the joy I feel when that same anointing that flowed out of Jesus flows out of me to others. It's miraculous! I'm not Oral Roberts or Benny Hinn. I'm just me! Jesus didn't use the learned. He used fishermen, a tax collector, and unlearned men!

I said, "God, if You could use a donkey (in the Old Testament), You can use me!" Because of what God has done for me, I am willing to be used for His glory, praise, and honor! If you are a born-again Christian, filled with the Holy Ghost, and desire to be used of the Lord, then say to the Lord: "**Lord, here I am! Use me for Your glory! Your will be done!**" He'll do it if your heart is in it because God is no respecter of persons! He will use the talent He has given to you if you don't hide it!

Moses had a speech problem and he felt unqualified to do what God had called him to do, but God gave him a helper, Aaron. And God still used him in spite of his imperfections because he was willing, and he was not drug down by his past. After all, he had been a murderer! But God gives us a new nature. We are new creatures in Christ Jesus when we are saved!

It has been prophesied to me by several ministers around the country that I would go into the nations and preach the gospel of the Lord Jesus Christ. I believe it and that is why I am writing this book, for when I can't go anymore because I am sixty-six years old, perhaps this book will continue going long after I've gone home to be with Jesus.

I pray it will help to win souls for Jesus, and to bring healing to men, women, and children, who have been abused; to help people who have had an encounter with demonic activity in their lives, not knowing a way out of their dilemma; to encourage people to follow after righteousness in Christ Jesus, and the leading of the Holy Spirit; to bring healing and deliverance to the oppressed.

For seventeen years, I have gone on the mission field. starting in Mexico. Now, I have gone into Central and South America with the Pentecostal Holiness World Missions. We build churches in three or four days. As few as sixty brethren and as many as ninety-three have gone on these mission trips. People give up their vacations and pay from their own pockets ($1,000.00) to go and build a church for the Kingdom of God.

I stand in awe many times as I watch the men all work together for the common goal for the Kingdom of God. I don't hear disputes or see fighting. Cursing is not heard. If a man is hurt, we gather around and cover him with prayer, which, in my seven years of going, very few times was anything more than a Band-Aid needed.

On a particular trip in Nicaragua, a huge board fell and hit a brother in the left arm. The male nurse who had come with the group sat him down and began to make a sling for his arm. I was told of the injury by a Nicaraguan woman, so I ran to pray for the brother. The nurse told me that the arm was broken! A small area on the top of his arm was raised a lot! I looked in the eyes of my brother and I declared with boldness, "Brother, I'm going to pray that your arm is not broken, and that it is only a bad bruise!"

The nurse replied, "Sister, can't you see that bone sticking up in the air?" I didn't reply, I just looked at my hurt brother and said, "I'm still going to pray that it is only a bad bruise. Okay?" The brother replied, "Sister, I agree with you, that it won't be broken because I have to go back to work!" I anointed him with oil, laid my hand lightly on the wound, and prayed the prayer of faith with him and called it "a done deal"! Thank You, Jesus, for Your healing virtue! Glory to God!

About an hour later, he came back from the hospital. He had to pay out $40.00 for an x-ray, which showed that he had a bad bruise! Almost all of the swelling was gone! Glory to God! And he went back to work! Miracles do happen when you pray!

God put it in my heart to walk around the building site while the cement block church was going up, interceding in prayer. Regardless of the heat, humidity, or whatever, even with swollen feet, I determined to do what I felt God told me to do! I have seen and heard of miracles as a result of the intercession that goes on for the group. I am not the only one who prays. There are many on the prayer team, and brethren who are at home holding down the fort, who participate in the move of God. Some of the men have told me how they appreciated me and my prayers, due to the fact that I could choose to sit in the shade and pray. But I choose to walk alongside of them as they work for the Lord.

One day in Panama, as I was walking around the building praying, I went into deep intercession. I started crying uncontrollably. I started thinking, *Oh, my God, I hope I don't scare some of these men and they drop a cement block on someone!* Later, they told me they knew I was in a battle in intercession. In fact, we were told later that five miles down the road from where the church was being built, was a witch coven doing their spells! After I stopped praying, black buzzards were flying in a circle over our heads. Immediately I thought of death! Needless to say, I continued praying until I received peace and death had passed over.

The following morning, a small group of the believers gathered together to have a time of devotion. The evangelist came hurriedly into the room and said, "You need to pray for me because I came under attack last night after going to bed. It felt like Satan was trying to choke me to death. I thought I was going to die, then suddenly it left my throat and I could breathe again!"

Instantly I knew what he had gone through. It had happened to me in the past. I went directly to him and said, "I want to pray for you because God has already revealed this to me!"

We all prayed for him and he received peace. Fear left him! (Intercessory prayer was working in his behalf!)

After the completion of every church we build, within three or four days there is a dedication of the building to God. Hundreds of people come to celebrate the occasion.

This particular night there were as many people outside the building as were inside. A young woman with her baby sat outside in a chair. All of a sudden, she handed her baby to her mother and fell onto the ground and died! The nurse outside was called over to her immediately. The nurse had just completed her CPR training before she left for the missions trip. With the help of the young woman's father, she started tending to her. The young woman had no pulse. She had stopped breathing and started turning blue. CPR was given and she came back to life! The next day, she was taken to the hospital and she was told she had a heart attack! Jesus brought her back because He wasn't ready for her to go to heaven yet! (Intercessory prayer was working!)

On the way home in the airplane, I was seated next to a pastor and his wife. I was asked to bless the food we had received. Before I said the blessing, as I bowed my head to pray, a grieving spirit of intercession came over me, and I said, "I can't right now. There is another need I have to pray about!"

The pastor told me to continue in my prayer, and he blessed the food. I continued praying until I received a peace, then I enjoyed my meal.

Upon arriving in Houston, Texas, before our next flight to Oklahoma, the pastor whom I had sat next to on the airplane was called over the intercom in the airport to call home – an emergency! He called home immediately and found out that his dad had had a heart attack and was in the hospital. Urgent! (Intercessory prayer was working!) When he arrived home, his father was doing better and lived a few more years before he went home to be with the Lord.

Intercessory prayer – there's nothing like it! But a born-again person must have open communication with Jesus and be sensitive to the leading of the Holy Spirit to fulfill the need of intercessory prayer.

After the evening work was over with the building of the church, crusades were held nearly every night while we were in that particular country at a mother church or out in the countryside! Many people come to hear the word of the Lord, and afterwards, we pray for the sick or whatever the needs are.

This particular night after the service, the group from Oklahoma was called up to pray for the people. Many people swarmed around us wanting us to pray for them. A woman with a small child grabbed my hand and asked me to pray for her daughter's ears. Not understanding completely everything in Spanish, even though I am learning, I just laid my hands on her ears thinking she might have an infection. I prayed the prayer of faith: "God, heal this precious little child in the name of Jesus!" Then, I went on to the next person.

At the end of the service, when everyone was about to leave, the woman with the little girl went up to the platform and spoke to the pastor. He cried out to the people, "Wait, she has a testimony she wants to share with the congregation!" She had taken her daughter to be prayed for at the altar, and prayer was received. Her daughter received a miracle! She was born deaf, and now she could hear! Glory to God!

A sister in Christ told me, "Emma, you prayed for that little girl!" Yes, I did, but I am not the Healer. Jesus is the Healer! We are His vessels through whom He can pour out His healing virtue to others for His glory!

During our lifetime, we lived in California a few times. At this particular time, we lived with different relatives. We had three of the children with us at that time. The two older children were at our home in Oklahoma.

Occasionally, I had the opportunity to go on the road with my husband cross country, who was a trucker at that time. I had the opportunity to experience what my husband went through as a truck driver for over twenty-eight years, all the pressures he had to go through both mentally and physically. I soon learned it wasn't all that easy to just sit and drive all day long. It gave me insight of the things he had to go through as a trucker. It takes an added strength from the Lord to be a Christian and a trucker too.

There are so many temptations along the road wanting to take you away from the Lord and to destroy you. I can say truthfully that while I was on the road with my husband, I was asked several times if I needed a ride somewhere by other truckers. I politely said. "No, I'm waiting on my husband to fuel, etc." I realized it was a hard life mentally, physically, and spiritually, but this is the road he chose and he provided for his family in this way. I thank God for him doing that, even though for countless days and nights for those twenty-eight years, I raised the family of five alone, not knowing Jesus almost all of that time. It was a hard row to hoe.

On a particular trip from California back East, I was with my husband. As we drove across the state of Arkansas one Friday morning, I started praying in the Spirit (in tongues) as I lay in the bunk bed. I went into deep intercession and prayed for a long time. I started weeping and weeping before the Lord and in a vision, as I was in prayer, I saw myself in a hospital bed covered with blood all over me!

How do I see this? It's like I'm watching television and different slides or pictures pass before my eyes for a few seconds. I am only shown these things as I am in prayer before the Lord. I believe it is perhaps a word of knowledge, or a word of wisdom, given to me by the Lord so I will pray concerning the issue.

Anyway, the second thing I saw was my husband. He sat in a chair by my side uninjured. I knew then to pray more! I didn't have fear, but I knew I needed to pray until I got peace over this situation. I knew then we would be in an accident, but I didn't know how or when it would happen, so I just continued to pray!

Little did I know, until I returned back to California, that during this same time, my brother-in-law, Andres, woke up his wife Francis (my husband's sister we were staying with), and said to her, "Francis, wake up! Wake up! Emma is in trouble! Pray for her!" he said. Andres had been dreaming that I was in a truck alone, it was going down a mountain, and I was screaming, "Help! Help!" It woke him several times, and each time he went back to sleep, the dream reoccurred. So then Francis prayed for God to protect me. I praise the Lord that He had others praying for me and that Francis was obedient and prayed even in the midnight hour!

Meanwhile, as we were traveling on an Interstate highway that same evening, we started moving around a curve where another two-lane highway joined, making the four lanes into three.

At this particular time there were four semitrucks trying to get into the three lanes! No cars were around, and the truck behind us on the right side (my side) was indeed in a hurry. As he pressed onward, the new trucks he was hauling crosswise the trailer, smashed against the cab of our truck. The outside handles of the cab, the bunk, and the mirrors were smashed in. Glass was flying everywhere!

This was one time that my window was up, I didn't have my arm hanging out of the window, and my safety belt was on! Thank God!

Then I screamed, "We're going to crash!" By that time, the tires were close enough for both trucks to collide with each other! At the sound of my voice, Oscar turned the wheel left with a fast jerk to get free of the truck on our right side, but he almost hit the tanker to the left!

Suddenly, two of the trucks came to a screeching halt! The tanker continued on out of danger. Praise God! There was an off ramp that the other trucker had pulled into to give everybody more room to stop!

One by one we went to the off ramp into a truck stop where the law was called. No one was issued a ticket because, as the law officer said, "So many accidents occur in that area and it's no one's fault!"

It sure taught me a couple of things, though. One, that I had better be prepared to go to meet the Lord at all times, and also that the devil can't take my life as long as God has His hand on me! Praise God! His hand was on us, and no one got hurt! I know God answered my prayer of intercession, and only God knows how many others He had praying for me at that time.

At one period of our life when we lived in California, we stayed with my husband's brother, Chuy, and his family in Huntington Park. They lived within walking distance of a very good Spirit-filled church. When my husband was on the road, I frequently visited the church, especially during the days when they had intercessory prayer.

One morning while Chuy was on his way to work, instead of me walking to the church, Chuy offered to give me a ride. I thanked him and accepted the ride.

On the way, as he drove down the street, he came up behind a car that had a young man sitting in the backseat. The young man had his hands high over his head, shaking all over. His head was moving back and forth without control. Chuy said to me, "Look Emma. It looks as if that boy is having a seizure!" I said, "Yes, I think so too!" As he started around the car to pass it, I looked at the young man and all of a sudden it rose up in me and out of my mouth came, "Spirit of epilepsy, in the name of Jesus Christ of Nazareth, I bind you, I rebuke you, and I command you to leave him, never to return! I have power and authority over you, you evil spirit, in the name of Jesus!"

A few seconds later, the young man's head completely stopped moving, his hands dropped down, and he relaxed. It was all over!

Chuy's mouth flew open, and he said, "Emma, did you see that?" I said, "Yes, God just set that young man free of that evil spirit! He'll never suffer from those seizures anymore!"

We then reached the church and I got out of the car, rejoicing in being able to see the manifestation of God working in someone's life and being a part of it! I called that one "a divine appointment"! Who knows, someone had probably been praying in his behalf for years for that miracle to happen. I believe it! These things just don't happen to be happenstance! It was God's divine plan!

Again, I got blessed by taking another trip with my husband on the road. Our relatives took care of our children (three were in school during the day) for us while we were gone. I always enjoyed going on the road with him. He would always say I went with him for the buffets at the truck stops and it was another vacation for me!

I enjoyed reading the Bible and talking while he did the driving. I sat up front and pretty soon I dosed off. I would wake up after a short spell, and he was still driving along hour after hour! I loved traveling across the United States with him and seeing God's beautiful country. In the Eastern states during the fall seasons, I beheld the most beautiful array of colors in the bounty of the trees. You could just imagine the awesome glory of God displaying His creation of splendor throughout the land. The snow-capped mountains and tall trees seemed to reach into the heavens and spoke of God's magnificent handiwork. I took every opportunity to go with Oscar so I could spend time with him and enjoy God's creation.

As I spent time in the truck with my husband, while driving down the highways sometimes God would give me poems and songs to write. Going to Hayward, California, on another trip, God gave me this poem for my husband. I want to share it, because now it is answered prayer.

My husband, a professional trucker, over the road grows weary and tired of carrying the load.

For twenty-four years he's beaten the path, to many distributors east and west.

Over the deserts, mountains, and valleys below, through the rain and snow-slick highways he must go.

Destined and determined, he must apply his strength, knowledge, and wisdom for the tasks thereby.

Though sickness and peril may strike at any time, he rests in the faith of the Lord Jesus, and no fear enters his mind.

A faithful servant to God he must be, and through the sweat of his brow, to his company.

But I have been praying for many a year, that God would bring him home and he would be near.

Five children we have, all grown and moved away, but with the love of God in our hearts, we were sustained this way.

He missed many a blessing while the children were home, but now those days are past and we won't dwell on.

Grandchildren are coming that Grandpa will enjoy, for I know my Lord Jesus, my prayers He will employ.

As I commit my ways unto Him and trust the Lord for the time, He says He'll save, heal, deliver, and restore all that is mine.

So, now is the time, I give God all glory and praise, for the answers to my prayers are on the way!

Answered Prayer, July 2000. Oscar has changed roles from a trucker to an ESL teacher! Glory to God! He ministers to Mexicans and other nationalities every day, teaching English as a second language. At home, after twenty-eight years on the road.

Now, one last trip experience. On this trip, we went to New Orleans, Louisiana. We were held over for the weekend since there were no loads for us to pick up or to deliver that Friday night.

We spent the night in a motel, and waking up bright and early Sunday morning, Oscar said to me, "Let's find a good church!" Immediately I grabbed the phone book, looked up churches near where we were, called them up, and they gave us directions on how to get there. So Oscar unhooked the trailer and we went to church in a big rig! Sometimes it was difficult to get in and out of those church parking lots, but where there is a will, there is a way!

What can I say about the church of Philadelphia? I hadn't been in such a church as that one! The praise and worship was wonderful. The people had such liberty to worship God and do what God wanted them to do without caring what someone else would say or think! I'm still talking about praise and worship.

The whole congregation raised their arms to the Lord in praise. There were people marching and dancing in the aisles. I had never seen this nor was I a part of this type of worship. (This was like twenty years ago!) I loved it! I couldn't wait to get back home to tell of this beautiful experience with the move and presence of God!

Tongues and interpretation and prophecies went forth as they waited upon the Lord. It seemed like there were at least five or six times when the Lord spoke! The praise and worship of God lasted over an hour or more. It was such a time of refreshing.

No one was in any hurry to stop the flow of the Holy Spirit. They didn't put a clock on the presence of God! It was after one o'clock before we left that church. But, we knew we had been to church!

During Sunday school that morning, there were about twenty brethren there. The teacher asked if there were any testimonies that someone wanted to share with the group. He shouldn't have said that! Not when I'm around, because I love to tell what God has done for me and what He is doing.

After a few testimonies were given, I raised my hand to tell my experience with Jesus and to give Him glory. Time flew by as I gave my testimony, and I believe God directed every word from my mouth. Several brothers and sisters came up to me and said that my testimony really ministered to them and lifted them up. It also gave them hope and answers to some of the situations that they were in that I had already gone through. Not only does God bless others through you, but He always blesses you, too, at the same time.

A young Christian girl came up to me and confessed that she had been harassed by demons every night in her room, and even though she called out in Jesus' name, they would leave but they would come back! She was living in tremendous fear, and she was keeping this to herself. She was afraid to share this problem with anyone else because very few people would understand what she was going through to be able to help her. Most people don't believe what you are trying to convey to them. But as the saying goes, "I've been there and done that!" So God sent us there to help her come out of that bondage of fear and torment! God will do that for even one person whom He loves very much to show that person that He cares!

While we were at that church, I had the opportunity and privilege to counsel and pray with her over this situation and show her how, in the name of Jesus, the blood of Jesus, the authority of Jesus, the power of Jesus, and the written Word of God, she could be set totally free forever of any more harassment!

I always experience a lifting up and a great joy within my spirit and soul as I minister the love of Jesus Christ to someone else regardless of their need. I found out that God will use me in this way if I am obedient to do what He tells me to do. It is such a joy to serve my Lord!

It was at this place, the church of Philadelphia, that a packet of tracts, a newsletter from the pastor of the church, etc. were handed to me and my husband upon entering the church.

As we got back in the truck after church was over, I glanced at a booklet and on the back of it was Revelation 3:7-8:

And to the angel of the church in Philadelphia write; These things saith he that is holy, he that is true, he that hath the key of David, he that openeth, and no man shutteth; and shutteth, and no man openeth;

I know thy works: behold, I have set before thee an open door, and no man can shut it; for thou hast a little strength, and hast kept my word, and hast not denied my name.

As I meditated upon the Word of God, He was showing me He had an open door for me. As I remembered back when I got saved and set free, the scripture that had been given to me by a Christian was that I was as Joshua was!

How was Joshua? I started reading the whole book of Joshua over again so I could receive the nugget God had for me. After we arrived home, during testimony service at another church, the pastor of the church said that my testimony was so interesting I should write a book! And once again, as I was watching Trinity Broadcasting Network, Pastor Jerry Barnard, hosting the night program, looked into the television camera. and said, "If anyone out there has a testimony, **write** a book!" Another confirmation that I needed to do this!

Upon completion of that portion of the Bible, I read how Joshua wrote a book! This indeed inspired me to continue writing this book, but I had not completed it because I felt it might not have been the right timing. It is necessary to be on God's time, not mine!

Now, many years later, through many confirmations of pastors, evangelists, and the Word of God, it is time to publish the wonderful things God has done in my life.

I don't shed tears of pain, sorrow, or fear anymore. I have been to the pit of hell, but now I am reaping *tears of joy* because Christ is in my heart and life.

Ephesians 6:11 says, **"Put on the whole armour of God, that ye may be able to stand against the wiles of the devil."** Remember, he is a defeated foe, and greater is He who is in you than he who is in the world!

Perhaps what I went through will give you the strength to say, "If she went through that, with God's help, so can I!" God's Word says, **"I can do all things through Christ which strengtheneth me"** (Philippians 4:13).

Lean not on your own understanding, but trust Jesus. Isaiah 10:27 says, **"And it shall come to pass in that day, that his burden shall be taken away from off thy shoulder, and his yoke from off thy neck, and the yoke shall be destroyed because of the anointing."**

God bless you as you read this book, which God put in my heart years ago. If only one person in this world gets plucked out of hell as a result of it, it is worth it!

As I am faithful in the prisons to pray the sinner's prayer for the women, I'm going to print it here also. If you desire to be a child of God by accepting Jesus Christ as the Lord and Savior of your life, please pray this prayer with me:

Dear Heavenly Father: I come to You as a sinner. I ask You to forgive me of all of my sins in my thoughts, words, and deeds. Cleanse me by the precious blood of Jesus of all unrighteousness and iniquity. I know that You, Jesus, are the Son of the living God. I know that You died for me, You were resurrected, and You sit at the right hand of the Father. With the confession of my mouth and believing in my heart, I accept You as my Lord and my Savior. I renounce and denounce Satan in my life. Leave me,

Satan, for I am no longer your child. I am a child of God, and I am on my way to heaven. Thank You, Jesus, for hearing my prayer and saving me, in the name of Jesus I pray. Amen and Amen!

I give Jesus all the glory, praise, and honor, and I thank Him for the anointing that He put on me to write this book.

Numbers 6:24-27 NKJV says:

"'The Lord bless you and keep you; the Lord make His face shine upon you, and be gracious to you; the Lord lift up His countenance upon you, and give you peace.' So they shall put My name on the children of Israel, and I will bless them."

I want to share a special song with you that God gave me, because it speaks of these end times we are living in. I pray it will minister to you as it has to me:

Jesus Is Coming in Glory

The dark clouds opened and my Lord appeared, riding on a white horse full of fury and fear.

Crowns on His head, wrapped in glory divine, on His way to earth, to fulfill the prophetic sign.

Angels surrounded Him, their wings spread in full array, flying with their Master, to Him they obey.

Saints in white followed Him, as He led the way. Victory was in sight, for there was no delay.

Jesus is coming in glory, for one or all, when the trumpet sounds, when the trumpet sounds, will you rise to the call? When the trumpet sounds, when the trumpet sounds, will you rise to the call?

The time is now upon us, saints, for the Lord's return to earth. Are you watching and praying that you may escape the dearth?

Rise up ole slumbering soul, your deliverance is nigh; be ready and alert for the sound of the cry.

Jesus is coming in glory, for one or all, when the trumpet sounds, when the trumpet sounds, will you rise to the call? When the trumpet sounds, when the trumpet sounds, will you rise to the call?

I believe God is telling us in this song, **Be ready, for Jesus' return is near!**

Here is another poem I want to share with you that the Lord blessed me with in December 1987:

I love the Lord Jesus, He lives within my heart.
To me He always tells me, He will never depart.
Even at times when I've failed Him,
And thought to be in the wrong,
He shows me His enduring love is forever strong.
He comforts me and encourages me
when times look bleak and dim,
By His strong hand of righteousness, He lifts me up to Him.
He says, "My child, fear not, the evil that is around,
For when you are under My wings, no evil can abound!"
So as I learn to trust in Him, my faith grows even stronger.
I will walk with Jesus, till I am here no longer.
He has given me life when this world has only death to offer,
I praise the Lord Jesus, for only through Him will I prosper.
He has given me many blessings, too numerous to count,
But life everlasting with Him,
is more valuable than the mount.
As we will enter in a New Year soon, a New Beginning, I see,
And with Jesus at the helm, victory will He give to me.
So as I look unto Him daily and say

Encouragement to Evangelize

He's my strength and my source,
He will guide me through all my problems
and I will have no remorse.
As each day brings new trials and troubles,
I know they will come,
But with the Lord Jesus by my side,
my battle has been won!
Amen! **Glory to God!**

Now, here is my testimony for the Hispanic population to read and to be blessed:

Ahora en estas ultimas paginas de mi libro, yo quiero y deseo concluir con mi testimo?o personal en Espanol.

Mi Testimonio Personal

Mi nombre es Emma Lou Hernandez y vivo en Oklahoma City, Oklahoma, U.S.A. Soy una ama de casa, quise venir a Mexico y otros paises, para compartir el amor de Cristo con ustedes. Ha sido mi anhelo por años de hacer esto, y ahora Dios me ha dado la oportunidad de poder venir a compartirlo con ustedes.

Durante 33 años, pertenecí a la religion de Testigos de Jehova. Ahora soy Cristiana.

No entendía que estabá condenada al infierno, pues mi religion no me ofrecía la seguridad de la vida eterna con Jesús.

Analicé que estaba perdida, enferma, con al azucar baja y úlceras por 21 años, hasta que Jesucristo me sanó.

Tuve una maldición de brujería por mas de 21 años.

Nadie me podia ayudar, pero sabía que en alguna parte alguien podria hacerlo, alguien superior al hombre. No tenía deseos de vivir, pues vivía en el pecado, odiaba mi vida.

Vino una persona y me dijo que era necesario que me arrepintiera de mis pecados, que invitara a Cristo a mi corazón, como mi Señor y Salvador. Lo hice, El me escuchó mi oración y cambió mi vida. Jesucristo nos ama y nos dá la libertad de escoger, y arrepentirnos.

El nos acepta como seamos, nos limpia de pecado, con su preciosa sangre y nos dá la vida eterna con solo pedir: "Señor ven a mí." Así nos lo dice en **Juan 3:16: "PORQUE DE TAL MANERA AMO DIOS AL MUNDO QUE HA DADO A SU HIJO UNIGENITO PARA QUE TODO AQUEL QUE EN EL CREE, NO SE PIERDA MAS Y TENGA VIDA ETERNA."**

El resultado de que Jesucristo haya entrado a mi vida, es que me cambio la vida, de una vida penosa, de miedo, odio, rechazo y de culpabilidad, a una vida de alegría, paz y amor que no se puede conocer sin el amor de Jesucristo. A la edad de 16 años fuí violada bestialmente durante una "cita a ciegas". Salí corriendo y gritando pero no había nadie que me ayudara. La biblia dice en Deuteronomio 22:25–27, que "si una virgen se encuentra en el campo y un hombre viene y la deshonra y ella grita pero no hay nadie que le ayude, Dios no la considerara culpable." Esta Sagrada Escritura ha levantado el peso de este incidente sobre mi. Y fui sana de esa hevida Gloria a Dios.

Despues del matrimonio con mi esposo por 47 años, fuí victima de una maldición de brujeria sobre mi y mi familia por 21 años. Vivíamos en tremendo terror todas las noches sin importar donde vivíamos. Los Demonios trataban de matarnos. No conociamos el poder ni la autoridad que el nombre de Jesucristo nos da si somos Hijos de Dios. No había ningun adivino, psiquiatra, sacerdote, familiar, ni Testigo de Jehova que nos pudiera ayudar. No había mas que una solución, y su nombre es JESUCRISTO! En ese tiempo no eramos salvados. Jesucristo y su palabra no era parte de nuestras vidas y sin embargo tuvimos que sufrir por nuestra ignorancia. Pero, en el tiempo de Dios, me arrepentí de todos mis pecados y recibí a Jesucristo como mi Señor y Salvador. Yo renuncié a todo lo que pertenece a satanas y su reino. Luego quemé toda la literatura de los Testigos de Jehova en mi chimenea, y esa noche todo lo malo se fue de mi casa. Todo el miedo y tormenta nos dejó. El nos salvo de la maldición. Oro para que la persona que puso tal maldición contra nosotros, sea salvada. Perdono a quien fue culpable y que Dios lo guie por el buen camino. El puso su mano sobre nosotros y no permitió que satanas nos matara! Ahora yo tengo este testimonio de todas las cosas maravillosas que Dios ha hecho en mi vida. El sanó mis enfermedades imediatamente por medio de una oración de un evangelista en una iglesia llena del Espiritu Santo. Y fui sanada por la sangre de Cristo.

Antes de ser salvada, pase por otro abuso recibí una golpiza que me hizo tener un ataque al corazón y mi cuerpo quedó paralizado de mi lado derecho desde mi cabeza hasta los dedos de pie. Yo grite, "Dios Jehova, ayudame!" Con dolor grave en mi pecho, mi espíritu salió de mi cuerpo. Ademas como ciertas personas dicen, tuve una experiencia fuera de mi cuerpo. Estabá en una bata blanca, volé dentro de un tunel muy obscuro a una tremenda velocidad. No habiá angeles, paz ni Gloria que me encontraran. Ni Jesucristo que me encontrara al final del tunel. Nadamas habiá obscuridad! Afuera en el celeste, con muchisimas estrellas, planetas y con una montaña que tenìa una mano que se veìa muy maliciosa, salió quitó la tapa y vino hacia mí para agarrarme! Grité y dije "la mano me va agarrar!" Inmediatamente fuí para atras en mi cama y por mi condición no podia hablar. Yo no creía en el infierno ni en el cielo. Nada mas sabía que no era muy buena para ser una de los 144,000 Testigo de Jehova que dicen que van ir al cielo. Yo le doy gloria a Dios porque Jesucristo ha hecho el camino por mi para que yo pueda ir al cielo. Yo no tengo que trabajar por el porque Jesucristo es el camino, la verdad y la vida. Mi hijito leyó el Salmo 34:1–22 en la biblia. Rapidamente el poder de Dios me sanó. Dios tiene un plan para que yo viva y no muera. El quiso que yo predicara la palabra de nuestro Señor Jesucristo.

Ahora soy una ministra ordenada. Yo le he servido fielmente por mas de 23 años. El puso el fuego del Espíritu Santo en mi y ahora soy Testigo de Jesucristo. Jesucristo me puso en el camino de las Misiones hace 17 años. He ído a México, Panama, Honduras, Cuba, Haití, Nicaragua, y muy pronto voy a ir a Ecuador. He estado sirviendo a Jesucristo en el sistema de prisiones por mas de 15 años en México, Texas y Oklahoma. En Oklahoma he predicado la palabra de Dios durante 13 años a las mujeres en la prisión.

Ha sido un honor y privilegio para mi servir al Padre, Hijo y Espiritu Santo que me aman. No puedo agradecer lo suficiente por todo lo que han hecho por mi. Quiero compartir a otros lo que El me ha dado a mi: su amor incondicional, misericordia y gracia. Le doy a Dios la Gloria porque le dio a mi familia y a mi otra oportunidad para vivir y proclamar su Santo Nombre a todo el mundo. Gracias a Dios.

Dios lo **Bendiga**.

AHORA, ESTE ES EL PLAN DE DIOS PARA LA SALVACION DE USTED.

¿Tiene Dios algún significado para su vida? (Deut. 10:17-18)

¿Sabe usted que Dios le ama? (Juan 3:16)

¿Jesucristo representa algo para su vida? (Juan 1:1)

¿Sabe usted que es pecador? (Rom. 3:10, 3:23)

¿Cree usted que Cristo murió por sus pecados? (Rom. 5:8, Juan 1:29)

¿Sabe usted que tiene que hacer con su pecados? La Biblia dice in 1 **JUAN 1:9, "SI CONFESAMOS NEUSTROS PECADOS, EL ES FIEL Y JUSTO PARA PERDONAR NUESTROS PECADOS, Y LIMPIAMOS DE TODA MALDAD."** ¿Cree usted esto?

ROMANOS 6:23 DICE: PORQUE LA PAGA DEL PECADO ES MUERTE, MAS LA DADIVA DE DIOS ES VIDA ETERNA EN CRISTO JESÚS SEÑOR NUESTRO." ¿Dese usted que Cristo Jesus le salve de sus pecados?

¿Que tiene que hacer? **APOC 3:20 DICE: HE AQUÍ, YO ESTOY A LA PUERTA Y LLAMO: SI ALGUNO OYE MI VOZ Y ABRE LA PUERTA ENTRARÉ A ÉL, CENARE CON ÉL Y ÉL CENARÁ CONMIGO. ¿QUIERE ABRIRLE A CRISTO LA PUERTA DE SU CORAZÓN HOY? HAGAMOS ESTA ORACION:** Oh, Dios, yo se que he hecho lo malo delante de ti y que te necesito. Gracias porque Cristo murió por mis pecados, y por medio de El, me ofrece vida eternal, te pido que me perdones y que me ayudes a no pecar contra tí. Acepto a Cristo Jesús como mi Salvador y le abro la puerta de mi corazón. Toma mi vida en tus manos, y hazla abundante y útil en el Nombre de Cristo, Amén.